AMAZING BUT TRUE!

150 Fascinating Stories About Canada

By Lowell Green

Spruce Ridge Publishing

Amazing But True!
150 Fascinating Stories About Canada

© 2017 Lowell Green

This book was researched, written, edited, designed, formatted, printed, delivered and sold in Canada by Canadians without any financial assistance from any level of government. In addition, HST in full has been paid at every level of production to editors, publishers, designers, artists, printers, delivery service, accountants, lawyers and advertisers. To the best of our knowledge, all paper used in this book was manufactured in Canada by Canadian pulp and paper workers. By buying this book you will not only know a good deal more about your country, but you will be contributing in no small way to provide jobs for Canadians.

SPECIAL THANK YOU TO LOCAL ARTIST JEREMY MILBANK FOR HIS BEAUTIFUL ARTWORK, INCLUDING THE WOMAN CLAD IN BEARSKIN ON THE FRONT COVER, AND TO THE MCP GROUP WHO DESIGNED, FORMATTED AND PRINTED THE BOOK.

Library and Archives Canada Cataloguing in Publication

Green, Lowell, 1936–, author
Amazing But True: 150 Fascinating Stories About Canada / Lowell E. Green

ISBN 978-0-9813149-5-2 (softcover)

1. Canada--Miscellanea. I. Title. II. Title: One hundred fifty fascinating stories about Canada. III. Title: One hundred and fifty fascinating stories about Canada.
FC60.G735 2017   971.002
C2017-901461-7

First Printing April, 2017

WHALES OVER OTTAWA

Did you know that huge beluga whales and goodness only knows what other sea creatures used to frolic right over top of Ottawa's Parliament Hill? Did you know that at one point Parliament Hill and much of Eastern Canada was buried under more than two miles of ice and snow? Or that many of our homes are sitting on top of ancient coral reefs?

The scientists who study these things tell us that there have been at least five ice ages during the past two and a half million years, but the one most of us know simply as "the Ice Age" peaked about 18,000 to 20,000 years ago and lasted the better part of 10,000 years. During this time these same scientists tell us the ice caps covering much of Canada, Russia and the southern part of South America were as much as 4,000 metres deep (12,000 feet). The glaciers knocked the tops off mountains and dredged out canyons, rivers and lakes.

The ice was so thick and heavy in the area roughly east of what is now Lake Ontario to the Atlantic Ocean that it actually compressed the earth, creating a kind of huge dent or sinkhole, in some cases hundreds of metres deep. Think of this—there was so much ice that the oceans were lowered by more than a 100 metres (400 feet.).

Starting about 11,000 years ago the ice began to melt (scientists aren't too sure why) with the water filling the big dent in the earth creating what we now call the Champlain Sea; it stretched all the way from roughly Kingston to the Atlantic and as far south as the southern tip of Lake Champlain in New York State. In fact,

Lake Champlain is pretty well all that is left of the Champlain Sea because, released from the weight of the ice, the earth began to slowly rebound, pushing most of the water back into the Atlantic Ocean. Most of the earthquakes occurring in Eastern Canada are in fact the earth still slowly rebounding from the weight of all that ice!

The whales cavorting over Parliament Hill are long gone, but the remains of the giant sea are everywhere in Eastern Ontario. Look to your right or left as you mount that little hill just east of Kanata, west of Ottawa. That grey rock you see is limestone, the remnants of an ancient coral reef.

Kingston calls itself the Limestone City but you would be hard pressed to find a single resident who knows that they are living in the midst of what was once one of the largest coral reefs in the Western Hemisphere.

CANADA 150

WHO'S FIRST?

Believe it or not, Canada was discovered and settled about 500 years before it was discovered!

No, this is not a typo! Most of us have been taught about Eric the Red and Lief the Lucky, but until fairly recently there was no real proof that the Vikings did indeed discover North America or that they settled here long before "14 hundred and 92 Columbus sailed the ocean blue".

That proof came in 1961 when Norwegian archaeologist Helge Ingstad discovered indisputable evidence that in about 1000 AD, a Norse settlement was established at what we now know as L'Anse aux Meadows in Newfoundland.

Those of us who have visited and been fascinated by L'Anse aux Meadows know it lies at the extreme northern tip of Newfoundland, about 25 kilometres from St. Anthony and is now a UNESCO World Heritage site.

There is no harbour there, but a tiny stream flows into the sea providing the early settlers with fresh water and a small meadow makes beaching a shallow draught boat possible.

The Norsemen were probably attracted to settle there by the great herds of whales and seals that pass nearby every year on their migration into the Gulf of St. Lawrence. (Yes, I checked and herds is the appropriate description of large numbers of whales and seals).

Around the turn of the 20th century, a Newfoundland historian argued that Viking sagas indicated there must have been a settlement in northern Newfoundland, but various archaeologists who examined the area found nothing.

The hunt was revived in 1960 when a Danish archaeologist searched the district which the local residents called "the Indian camp" but it wasn't until the following year that Ingstad uncovered relics of a small encampment of eight buildings, housing about 75 people which carbon dating placed at about the year 1000 AD, 400 - 500 years before North America was discovered!

A VERY FURRY STORY

Canada was founded, explored and developed mainly because of the fur trade. But did you ever wonder what they wanted with all those furs? It wasn't to cover fine ladies' backs you know.

By far the most important fur was beaver, sought, not for its warmth or glossiness, but for a unique feature of its hair. The beaver pelt is minutely barbed. This helps the animal trap a layer of air against its body for protection against the cold water. The little barbs are on the beaver's undercoat.

In preparing for commercial use, the long, outer guard hairs are first scraped off and the much prized short barbed wool-like fur beneath it is then used in the making of felt for the hat industry. That's right, the beaver in Canada was harvested by the thousands almost entirely to make top hats for fine gentlemen of the day!

Under the pressure of the felting process, the barbs hold the whole thing together better than any other material. Very often cheaper fur, such as rabbit or even cat is used, but always for the best quality hats, beaver is the fur of choice.

A beaver hat was the hat of fashion. Stiffened by shellac, it was moulded into the famous top hat, the tricorne or the flat shape, according to the vogue of the day. Of course other furs such as mink, marten, ermine and fox were also trapped and in considerable demand, primarily for female fashion, but it was the beaver fur that dominated the trade and played such a major role in Canada's development—all for the sake of man's vanity!

WHAT'S IN A NAME?

In late 1759, Voltaire once described Canada as a "few acres of ice and snow". But we may in fact have obtained our name from a few disgruntled Spanish explorers who described our country as a place of nothing.

There's a good deal of dispute of course. The original name to identify Canada is generally believed to be the Iroquois word Kanata or Kanada, meaning a cabin or lodge. This name makes its first appearance in Cartier's account of his second voyage in 1535, but there is also a possibility that the name originated with Spanish explorers who failed to find gold mines here and described the country by the Spanish phrase—"Aca-nada", Aca meaning here, nada meaning nothing, thus nothing here.

Katherine Livingston MacPherson of Montreal has included this explanation in a poem which says:

> *"Long ago, a band of seamen left behind the coast of Spain.*
>
> *Drove their craft through gale and spindrift; sailed the storm-swept trackless main.*
>
> *Sternly sought an Eldorado, where the northern cliffs appear.*
>
> *Fondly hailing hope's bright vision, gold the only guerdon dear.*
>
> *Reckless flung a tropic halyard—"ACA NADA— NOTHING HERE".*

MEANER THAN A
JUNKYARD DOG!

The second attempt at founding a colony in Canada failed as miserably as the first, thanks in part to a public hanging and the terribly cruel treatment of a pair of star-crossed lovers!

When Jacques Cartier returned to France in 1541, without his sought after treasures of gold and jewels following three trips to Canada, his career was pretty well over.

The next man to try and find the mythical Kingdom of the Saguenay with its rumoured incredible riches was that cruel pirate, Jean-Francois de La Rocque de Roberval. Yes Roberval, the man whose name Quebec towns and institutions still bear. A man so mean and cruel it destroyed his chances of finally establishing a permanent colony at Stadacona, near or perhaps at what is now present day Quebec City.

When Roberval arrived at Stadacona he found two forts built by Cartier but abandoned. He added several more buildings, cleared some fields and sent some of his men inland to try and find the gold and diamonds some native Indians claimed could be found in the mysterious "Kingdom of the Saguenay."

The colonists, already deeply disturbed by Roberval's banishment of his niece and her young lover onto what was then known as "the island of demons" grew to hate Roberval. He ordered frequent floggings and other cruel punishments for the slightest offence and worked the men and women until they fell from exhaustion.

Some kind of open rebellion broke out. The ringleader was caught, whipped until almost dead then publicly hanged.

Completely demoralized, the few who survived the punishments, the work and scurvy, sailed for home the following summer, leaving behind only a few buildings to mark this visit of the white man to the Canadian wilderness of the St. Lawrence Valley.

For a time at least Canada was returned to the natives, and incredibly—Roberval's niece left alone on that cold deserted island!

MIRACULOUS SURVIVAL ON THE ISLAND OF DEMONS

The beautiful young Marguerite de La Rocque paid a terrible price for falling in love!

We don't know her lover's name, probably because he was a member of the French aristocracy whose members wished to avoid the notoriety. We do know that Marguerite was a very wealthy noblewoman, beautiful, young and unmarried but had the misfortune of being related to the cruel pirate Roberval. Why she accompanied Roberval on his 1542 voyage to "The New World" is unknown. What kinds of promises were made or what Roberval's intentions were we can only surmise.

But for some reason when Roberval discovered that Marguerite had taken a young man as a lover aboard ship, he flew into a rage and banished both of them along with Marguerite's maid-servant Damienne onto a deserted island off the northern tip of Newfoundland. An island believed to be filled with evil spirits and wild beasts that attacked any approaching ships, known by explorers as Ile des Demons (the island of demons or spirits).

The Island is known today as part of the "Isles de la Demoiselle", presumably in recognition of Marguerite. It is called Hospital or Harrington Island where locals can show you the cave where Marguerite lived for several years.

How many years she survived on that desolate island is unclear, some historians say two years—others say longer. Tragically, most of the time she was entirely alone. Her lover and her maid-servant both died before she gave birth on the floor of that small cave. Half-starved, she was unable to produce sufficient milk to keep the baby alive. It died weeks old in her arms.

Although raised in luxury and privilege this young woman kept herself alive by hunting rabbits, birds and the occasional seal with the firearms and knives Roberval had left with her. When found years later by Basque fishermen, she was wearing the hide of a bear she had obviously shot and skinned.

Anyone who has spent a winter in Northern Newfoundland can well imagine the cold and storms she endured.

Returning to France after her rescue, Marguerite achieved some celebrity when her story was published by the Queen of Navarre, then later by several other authors.

Her incredible story of courage and survival has been the subject of many more recent books, plays, and even TV documentaries.

What seems to have been lost in most of the recounting is the fact that in all probability for a while at least, Marguerite de La Rocque was the only white person alive in all of North America!

CANADA 150

FINALLY CANADA IS BORN!

It is the third attempt at colonizing Canada that finally succeeds, but only after tremendous hardship and death and a murderous plot!

Jacques Cartier was the first to attempt to establish a colony on the banks of the St. Lawrence River near what is now Quebec City. The tiny settlement failed after just one miserable, deadly winter. Roberval's attempt the following year was no more successful. So for about 60 years Canada was visited only infrequently by Europeans picking up loads of furs from the native Indians and by fishermen on the Grand Banks just off Newfoundland.

In our wildest imaginations few of us today can even contemplate packing a few possessions, boarding a space craft and heading off for Mars, leaving behind our friends, relatives and way of life, never to return to earth again. And yet, when you think about it, that's pretty well the fate that faced those first few brave souls who left everything behind for the perilous voyage to the "New World" which was, in no small way, the Mars of those long ago days.

When old Samuel de Champlain sets sail in 1608, many people still believe the earth is flat and if you sail too far you will drop over a giant cliff into nothing. Stories of giant sea serpents, dragons and other wild beasts are generally accepted as true.

Thus it was that when Champlain makes his historic voyage and establishes the first permanent colony in Canada, at what is now Quebec City, he is joined by only 27 (some historians say 32 or even 38) colonists prepared to make a life in what is then called "New France". That's right, believe it or not, Canada is founded on July 3, 1608 when Sam Champlain plants the French flag on the banks of the St. Lawrence River surrounded by fewer than 40 brave souls, most of whom die during their first "Canadian" winter.

What a terrible winter it is. They haven't been able to grow sufficient crops to tide them through until the spring and local native Indians for some reason have little luck trapping or hunting for wildlife. Scurvy breaks out and one by one the colonists become ill and die.

In the midst of all this misery a man named Jean Duval begins to hatch a plot to murder Champlain whom he blames for their misfortune. He might very well have succeeded thus completely changing Canada's early history but one of the tiny band blows the whistle on the deadly plot.

Duval is hanged for his efforts and his head placed for a while atop the flagpole.

But by the time spring arrives only eight of that small group have survived. The ship's pilot a man named Laroute, two boys, Etienne Brule, Nicolas Marsolet, Champlain and two others whose names have been lost in history.

Eight starving but hardy survivors, who it can honestly be said, were the first Canadians.

When Champlain dies in 1635 in the colony he founded, the population has grown to 250 and is soon to grow much larger thanks to "The Daughters of the King"!

THE KING'S DATING SERVICE

Yes, it's true, Hillary Clinton, the woman who almost became President of the United States is descended from one of those who took part in a highly successful dating service established by French King Louis XIV way back in 1663. They called the women who took part, Les Filles du Roi, or in English, Daughters of the King, but it really was what is probably the world's first dating service, intended to hook up about 800 unmarried French women with lonely colonists in far off "New France". And hook up they did—usually in a big hurry!

Hillary Clinton can trace her ancestors back to a marriage between Fille du Roi, Madeleine Niel and a colonist named Ducorps in 1664. She is not alone in this regard. Movie star Angelina Jolie is a descendent of Les Filles du Roi, Denise Colin. Madonna can trace her roots back to Les Filles du Roi, Anne Seigneur. Hall of Fame hockey player Bernie "Boom Boom" Geoffrion was a direct descendent of Marie Priault, a King's Daughter and Pierre Joffrion, a farmer and former grenadier from the Careigan-Salieres Regiment. The pair married shortly after her arrival in 1669.

The "New World" in those early days was a man's world: Soldiers, farmers, fur traders, trappers and priests. The man in charge of New France, Jean Talon, came up with a brilliant marketing idea. Get the King to sponsor a few hundred women so they could keep the men on this side of the Atlantic, attract a few more and grow the population.

King Louis wasn't stupid. The burgeoning British colonies to the south were threatening his claim to ownership of the land along the St. Lawrence. "We need at least 500 single women here," said Talon. He got what he wanted and then some.

"Okay", said the King. "I'll pay 100 livres to the East Indian Company for every woman they transport to New France—each woman will get 400 livres as a dowry." (In those days a livre was equal in value to a pound of silver). The offer was so good that when Les Filles du Roi program ended in 1673, ten years after it was launched, almost 800 women, most between the ages of 12 and 25, had answered the clarion call from the King, thrown caution to the wind and headed across the bounding main for a new life in this new, raw land, usually with pretty raw men!

History is a bit confused when it comes to who was chosen first when the ships landed at what is now Quebec City followed by Trois Rivieres then Ville Marie (Montreal). Who was chosen first, the prettiest or the ones with strong legs for working the fields or wide hips for child bearing? What do you think?

The whole thing was amazingly civilized when you consider the time and the circumstances. The women had a right to reject any proposal and in fact while the great majority were married and pregnant within a year of arrival, several didn't find suitable mates for two or three years.

One of the problems was that most of Les Filles du Roi were from urban areas in France, poor but used to the city life. More than half were from Paris and had never seen a cow or pig, let alone snow or terrible cold. But with few exceptions they adapted, prospered and in no small way can be described as "the mothers of the Country."

Les Filles du Roi may not have been pretty or rich, but they were certainly fertile! In 1671—eight years after the first arrival, the Daughters of the King gave birth to nearly 700 babies and by 1672 the population of New France had risen to 6,760 from 3,200 in 1663.

THE LITTLE NURSE

Some history books may disagree, but a growing number of people now believe the true founder of Montreal was a little nurse.

From childhood, Jeanne Mance was deeply religious. At age seven she took the vows of poverty and chastity, although for some unknown reason she never took the veil, instead studied to become a nurse.

At age 34 Jeanne was a delicate looking woman with dark eyes, long black curls and classically beautiful features. A priest stirred her imagination with tales of service in the new religious colony being established at Ville Marie, now Montreal. With assistance and funding from friends in France she made the momentous decision to found a hospital in the wilderness of New France.

It was May of 1642 when she arrived in Ville Marie, occupied then by a handful of hardy colonists who were under almost constant attack by Iroquois Indians. Immediately, Jeanne began directing the construction of a hospital.

The foundation was barely laid when the Indians attacked again inflicting death and terrible wounds on several. Jeanne's first patient was a man who had been scalped. History doesn't tell us whether he survived.

Jeanne managed to complete the hospital but for 11 years the colony was still threatened by Indians until Governor Paul de Chomedey Sieur de Maisonneuve decided to abandon the settlement and take the few survivors back to France. He had been badly shaken by a recent battle during which he killed an Indian chief with his bare hands!

In an act of incredible bravery, Jeanne Mance told Maisonneuve that she would remain behind alone if necessary. "Go back to France," she told him, "there's a woman there who will give you enough money to hire some soldiers to bring back. Those of us who stay will hold off the Indians." And they did.

Months later a triumphant Maisonneuve returned with not only 100 soldiers but a number of settlers as well.

Jeanne became widely regarded throughout New France as a saint who could work miracles. Her reputation was enhanced when she launched the world's first medical pre-payment plan. Physicians at her Hotel Dieu Hospital agreed to dress wounds and care for the sick for 30 sous per year.

She laid one of the cornerstones of the beautiful Notre Dame Cathedral which still stands in old Montreal. She is portrayed in one of its stained glass windows; and lives on in the hearts of most Montrealers to this day.

THE SAINT

The great gateway to Canada bears the name of one of history's most venerated saints who died a horrible death to help the poor.

By sheer chance, Jacques Cartier sails into a little bay on the north shore of what is now the Gulf of St. Lawrence on the feast day of who else? St. Lawrence of course. So it is only natural that he names the little bay after the martyred saint.

The name quickly spreads to include the entire gulf and then the river and now the Seaway that stretches from Lake Superior to the Atlantic Ocean.

We know very little about Lawrence's background until he is appointed the first of seven deacons of the Catholic Church in ancient Rome by Pope Sixtus II. This is a position of great trust, including care of the treasury and riches of the Church and distribution of alms among the poor.

But only 258 years after the death of Christ it's a time of great danger for members of the fledgling Christian community. Romans are throwing Christians to the lions. Pope Sixtus II is put to death and the Prefect of Rome demands that Lawrence turn over the riches of the Church to him. The young deacon asks for three days to assemble all the treasures but instead begins distributing all the Church's wealth to the poor of Rome.

At the end of the three days Lawrence shows the Prefect dozens of the poor residents of Rome and according to several accounts says, "Behold in these poor persons are the treasures which I promised to show you, to which I will add pearls and precious stones, these widows and consecrated virgins, which are the Church's crowns."

The Prefect is so angry he has a great gridiron prepared with burning coals beneath it upon which Lawrence is placed, dying an extremely slow and painful martyr's death.

There are several churches in Rome today dedicated to him including San Lorenzo in Panisperna, the place where he was executed.

The gridiron, upon which it is believed he was martyred, is on display in the church of San Lorenzo in Lucina.

His celebration on August 10 has the rank of a feast day throughout the Catholic world.

It seems appropriate that one of the greatest rivers in the world is named for one of Christendom's greatest saints.

FISH, FISH AND MORE FISH!

Believe it or not, we can likely credit the Grand Banks of Newfoundland for the fact that most of North America speaks English and not Spanish, Dutch, Portuguese or French.

There is no question that the French were the first to settle Canada, but it was the British who colonized most of North America mainly because of the fish!

Let me explain. Huge fishing fleets, mostly British, were already reaping the harvest of the Grand Banks by the time Champlain founded Quebec. In fact, some historians believe fishermen may even have preceded Columbus and Cabot. By Champlain's time 300 ships were making the crossing each year. Crews in English ships alone numbered at least 18,000. The fish were so thick it is reported that upon occasion ships had difficulty making their way through the enormous schools. Small boats could scarcely get their oars into the water!

Historians believe that it was primarily the Banks fishery that built and sustained the British tradition of seamanship and ship building that enabled England to defeat the Spanish, the Dutch and the French. A naval supremacy was established that made possible British control over most of the North American continent.

Not only that. The rich cargoes of fish also provided food to feed the citizens back home which encouraged growth of the population. This in turn created fresh markets for other products of the New World, such as fur and timber and greatly encouraged the supply of new immigrants to North America, mostly from Britain.

The largest of the Banks lies southeast of Newfoundland where the Labrador Current and the Gulf Stream meet. The cold water is denser than the warm and sinks beneath it. Moving at this low depth, the submerged current stirs up the plankton at the bottom which attracts great schools of fish. Or at least it used to.

Man's greed and stupidity, as we all know now, almost wiped out the fish population through overfishing, especially with huge factory ships using their giant nets. Thanks to major conservation efforts, fish stocks on the Grand Banks are slowly recovering, but for more than 400 years they helped to feed the world of yesterday and helped to create the world in which we live today.

CANADA 150

MRS. BARTON

There are undoubtedly thousands of Canadians of English and Scottish ancestry who owe a great deal, perhaps even their very existence, to a plucky little Scotswoman whose first name we don't even know.

All we do know of her is that her name was Mrs. Barton. She came from the Scottish lowlands and set sail from Liverpool in 1840 bound for Canada. The ship was the small 400 ton "Nancy" with 312 aboard, 100 more than the law of the day allowed.

As was the case with most immigrants in those days, all but a privileged few travelled in the steerage, a long low corridor just five and a half feet high, 25 feet wide and about 75 feet long. No person had more than two feet of width in which to turn. You can just imagine how terrible conditions were!

Into this tiny space were jammed some 300 poor souls and all their belongings. Sanitary facilities were virtually non-existent. Most of the would-be colonists were seasick much of the time.

The death rate on trips such as this was often as high as 25 or 30 per cent. The dead were simply dumped overboard. More than 4,000 Irish died in the so called "coffin ships" that carried survivors of the potato famine to Canada!

But during Nancy's voyage, largely due to the efforts of Mrs. Barton, there was not a single recorded death.

Mrs. Barton made the women keep their quarters scrupulously clean and organized all the cooking to ensure sanitary procedures were followed. She insisted that the buckets used as toilets be emptied several times a day and thoroughly cleaned each time.

During one recorded terrible storm when all the hatches were battened down, Mrs. Barton persuaded some of the men to bring out their musical instruments and instead of the usual screams of fear, they danced and sang.

Mrs. Barton nursed the sick and prevented quarrelling. The ship's log is filled with praise for her.

We don't know her first name, or even where she settled, but it was immigrants like Mrs. Barton who helped make Canada great.

THE FIRST LAW

The first British law declared in what is now Canada was to ensure that everyone belonged to the right church! That church was, of course, the Church of England.

Most of us know that on August 5ᵗʰ, 1583 Sir Walter Raleigh's half-brother Sir Humphrey Gilbert sailed into what is now St. John's Harbour in Newfoundland and claimed the Island in the name of Queen Elizabeth I. It was a fascinating ceremony in front of a large tent.

Immediately upon landing, Gilbert sent out notifications to all those fishing off the Newfoundland coast and those drying their fish on shore that they must sail into the harbour and the captains and crews come ashore.

As an illustration of the popularity of Grand Banks fishing, no fewer than 36 vessels were assembled for the ceremony.

Gilbert handed to each of the captains a certificate allowing them to fish the area and use the harbour and other parts of the mainland for re-supplying or dropping cargo. To some captains he granted the right in perpetuity to use the land they needed to dry their fish on the rocky outcroppings. Incredibly, one of these special certificates turned up in Seville, Spain recently, where it is now featured in a museum. In return for these privileges the fishermen had to provide him sufficient fish to provision his ships which had run very low on food.

Then Gilbert was presented with a large piece of Newfoundland soil and a large wooden rod was driven into the ground with the Queen's coat of arms attached. In a loud commanding voice

Gilbert took possession of Newfoundland and "200 leagues north and south" for the Queen and proclaimed three laws to take effect immediately.

The first law stated that "all public display of religion in the newly claimed lands should be according to the Church of England." The second law said that, "any person trying to take the lands from her Majesty the Queen should be executed and in the case of high treason, according to the laws of England." Third, "if any person should utter words sounding to the dishonour of her Majesty, he should lose his ears and have his ship and goods confiscated."

Accompanying Gilbert on the expedition was one of England's leading experts in minerals who, after a few days exploring, claimed he had found large deposits of silver.

Anxious to return to England with the good news and several ore samples, Gilbert headed for home about two weeks after the ceremony. His haste cost him his life.

Gilbert's ship the Sparrow with all hands aboard, including his mineral expert and the samples, were lost in a vicious storm not far from Sable Island.

Almost until the end of the 20th century miners tried to find that silver without success. Lots of iron ore and other minerals but only a tiny speck or two of silver; however Newfoundland remained a part of the British Empire until joining Canada in 1949.

THE GRANDEST CANYON

Did you know that we have in Canada a canyon about three times wider than and nearly as deep as the famous Grand Canyon?

The reason you likely have never heard about Canada's huge canyon is because you can't see it, but it's there beneath the St. Lawrence River.

Our "grander" canyon starts a few miles east of Montreal but can't really be called a canyon until the mouth of the Saguenay River. There the St. Lawrence suddenly reaches a depth of 1,000 feet, gradually deepening and growing broader as it heads for the Atlantic Ocean.

By the time the River reaches the Gulf of St. Lawrence it is more than 50 miles wide and close to 2,000 feet deep.

If the water were to be drained it would present a sight far more spectacular than the Grand Canyon which is never more than 18 miles wide. Fact is, our canyon extends well beyond the outer limits of Canada's shoreline many miles out onto the Continental Shelf.

Our canyon runs along what is called Logan's Fault, essentially a crack in the earth's surface that occurred, a bit before you were born, about 450 million years ago!

The evidence is that a huge glacier, perhaps as high as five miles, plunged southward dredging out the Saguenay Valley until it struck what is now Anticosti Island which is made of very hard rock. This action deflected the ice eastward along the ancient

Logan's Fault, scooping out an ever deepening and widening canyon. When the ice finally melted the canyon filled with the water creating the mighty St. Lawrence River.

Now here's something else you probably don't know. Mainly because of this huge crack in the earth's surface, the banks of the St. Lawrence have moved an estimated two or perhaps three feet eastward since the Ice Age.

In fact, there is plenty of evidence that the cities of Montreal, Quebec City and maybe even Ottawa may be a few inches closer to the Atlantic today than when our grandparents were born!

BLACK CHAPTER

One of the saddest chapters in Canadian history is the story of how an entire race of human beings was wiped from the face of the planet.

The Beothuk, the native Indian tribe of Newfoundland, became extinct on June 6, 1829 when Nancy Shanawdithit died in St. John's, NL.

The campaign to eradicate her race was every bit as determined as the one which saw the passenger pigeon disappear from the face of the earth, even though, in all honesty, there was considerably more public concern over the last pigeon than the last Beothuk.

The Beothuk were an historic race, the first Indians ever seen by white men, first by the Vikings, then by Cabot. It was their custom of painting their bodies red that earned forever the name, "red skin" for all North American Indians.

A relatively peaceful tribe, they were nonetheless hunted like animals by white men and even by other Indians. Great hunting parties were held, sometimes with Micmac Indians from the mainland used as guides.

The Beothuk's only crime was that they considered all property as communal and often "borrowed" hunting and fishing equipment without asking the white villagers.

As their numbers dwindled, the colonial government launched a "Save the Beothuk" policy in the late 18th century but nothing was ever done to enforce the law. Not a single white man was ever penalized for killing a Beothuk.

As a last ditch attempt at saving the race from extinction, the government offered a reward of 50 pounds for the capture of a live Beothuk.

Tragically, it was too late. The only Beothuk still alive were three women, Nancy Shanawdithit, her mother and sister who were all captured at Badger Bay.

Both her relatives died shortly after capture, but Nancy lived, as the only representative of an entire race of human beings until June 6, 1829, at which time the Beothuk became extinct.

CANADA 150

ONE TOUGH WOMAN!

Davy Crockett may have killed a bear when he was only three, but Canada has a heroine who fought off hordes of Indians when she was only 12 and then again when she was 14!

Fighting Indians came naturally to Madeleine de Vercheres. When she was only 12, for two frightening days, she and her mother defended her father's fort near Montreal against a band of marauding Indians.

Two years later Madeleine found herself virtually alone as, once again, Indians attacked that same small fort on the south shore of the St. Lawrence, a few kilometres east of Montreal where today a beautiful statue of Madeleine graces the town square of Vercheres, QC.

As often occurs with accounts of our early history there are some conflicting reports of what actually happened, but this much is clear.

It is summer, 1692. A calm warm day. A group of between eight and 22 settlers leaves the Vercheres fort to work in nearby fields. Among them is 14 year old Madeleine Vercheres who by this time had already lost a brother and two brothers-in law to attacking Indians.

Suddenly from the nearby forest spring about 40 whooping Iroquois who capture all of the settlers except for Madeleine who manages to outrun them, dash into the fort and slam the gate behind her, yelling at the few inside to start firing muskets and make as much noise as they can.

Madeleine throws a soldier's helmet onto her head then fires a small cannon to alert nearby forts of the attack, a sound which for a few moments frightens the Indians into a brief retreat.

Inside the fort are only two soldiers, several children including her two brothers aged six and nine, an old man and several women. The soldiers are so frightened they are about to blow up the store of gunpowder and make a run for it but Madeleine persuades them and several women to run from loophole to loophole firing their muskets in an attempt to persuade the Indians there are dozens of soldiers inside. The children, including her brothers, re-load the guns.

Depending upon which account is to believed, the siege lasts between two and eight days before forces from nearby Montreal arrive and drive the attackers off. It is unclear what happened to the settlers who had been captured. One account claims they were all killed, another account says they were freed by the attacking soldiers, a third story is that they were rescued by other friendly Indians.

Incredibly, for a while, Madeleine comes under vicious attack by at least one cleric who claims that because she had assumed a man's role in the fight and even donned a man's helmet she must be a woman of low repute, but over the years most Quebecers have come to consider Madeleine de Vercheres one of their great pioneering heroes.

THE PRINCESS

There are few adventurous or romantic stories that can top that involving the birth of what is believed to be the first "white" baby born in Newfoundland to a woman everyone calls the Carbonear Princess.

The incredible story begins in Ireland when Sheila Nagira grows into such a beautiful young woman that her aristocratic family decides to thwart the young men flocking around by shipping her off to a convent in France run by her aunt.

Luckily for Sheila and Newfoundland she never sees the inside of that convent. A Dutch pirate ship attacks the vessel in which she is sailing. Many of the Irish sailors are killed, but Sheila is so beautiful the pirates decide to take her prisoner.

But the odyssey is far from over.

Several days after her capture, three British warships, on their way to Newfoundland spot the pirates and attack. There's a running battle lasting most of the day but Sheila is finally rescued, unharmed.

The British ships continue to Newfoundland and during the voyage, a bold young Lieutenant falls in love with Sheila and she with him.

They waste no time and marry on board.

They arrive in Newfoundland as Mr. and Mrs. Gilbert Pike and go to live in the little town of Carbonear near Conception Bay on the Avalon Peninsula, one of the earliest settlements in Newfoundland.

Everyone loves Sheila, especially the Irish fishermen who give her the name the Carbonear Princess because of her regal bearing and aristocratic birth. It is said the Pikes could have lived comfortably for the rest of their lives without ever having to work, so many gifts did the settlers bring to them.

When Sheila gives birth to what is believed to be the first "white" baby born in Newfoundland, people flock from one end of the Island to the other just to see the beautiful princess and her little prince.

Even to this day, residents of the area will tell you that never has there been anyone as kind, gracious and beautiful as their Carbonear Princess.

TOTEM POLE PRIDE

It's hard to believe but before the white man arrived on Canada's west coast, native Indians sometimes used tools made from beaver teeth to carve the beautiful and very artful totem poles that we so admire today. The rougher work was usually done with stone knives, but we now know that in some cases the carvers used tools fashioned from beaver teeth to complete the finer details. Steel, in fact metal of any kind, was unknown to indigenous people until the white man arrived.

Only Indians along the North American west coast carve totem poles, probably because the giant redwoods of their forests are soft enough to work with primitive tools.

The practice actually began hundreds of years before Captain Vancouver sailed up the west coast of Canada. At that time the Indians carved huge pillars required to support the ridge poles of their enormous longhouses which often soared more than 20 feet high (6 metres) and stretched for 200 or more feet (60 metres) in length.

Gradually, the carving evolved into a prestige symbol, with the various Indian families vying with each other for the most beautiful and symbolic poles. When the white man first arrived on the scene, about the year 1791, the carvers began to use steel tools and their skills improved immensely.

The totem pole, in many cases, is a kind of coat-of-arms for the West Coast Indian, representing the history and feats of his family and their social standing. The poles are usually of animals connected with the history of their ancestors. Sometimes they represent ideas, partly social and partly religious, concerning the relationship of man to other animals. But not always.

Some tribes fashioned special mortuary poles to bear the bodies of tribal leaders or elders. Memorial poles were often placed in front of houses in honour of deceased chiefs. The Coast Salish people in southern BC and western Washington State carved large human figures on their totem poles to represent ancestors and spirit helpers.

Many of the poles we see today, such as those in Vancouver's Stanley Park, display a high degree of artistic skills, comparable in some cases to some of the finest sculpting done in western cultures.

The totem pole of yesterday and today is in fact, an example of some of the finest original Canadian artistry available.

"Art," say many, "which at its best is fully comparable to Canada's famous Group of Seven."

THE BELCHER ISLANDS
MASSACRE

"I am Jesus", cries Charlie Ouyerak. "I am God", says Peter Sala and within days nine Inuit lie dead on the frozen ice of Belcher Island. It is one of Canada's most gruesome mass murders.

It's 1941, missionaries are hard at work in the far north trying to win souls for the Christian faith. The techniques do something to the mind of middle-aged Charlie Ouyerak. "I am Jesus," he claims. "They promise that Jesus is coming back to earth. I have seen visions and I now know I am Jesus."

Almost immediately another native of the Belcher Islands, Peter Sala, begins having visions of his own which convince him that he is God. A kind of religious frenzy overtakes many of the isolated natives.

Special revival meetings are held with Charlie and Peter continuing to claim they are Jesus and God to the shouted approval of the gatherings. But a 13 year old girl we know only as Sarah, isn't having any of it. "I know Charlie Ouyerak and Peter Sala and do not believe they are Jesus and God," she says.

The congregation, already whipped into hysteria, attacks Sarah and murders her. Another member of the growing cult, dismayed at what has happened, demands that this madness stop. He is shot and killed.

A few days later yet another Inuit comes to his senses and tells Charlie and Peter they have to stop what they are doing. A court of several believers is held during which it is agreed that this non-believer is the devil and must be killed.

But the gruesome insanity still doesn't end. Charlie's sister (or his mistress no one seems clear), a woman named Mina, one evening declares that she has just experienced a vision that the real Jesus is coming again and everyone must go outside to "meet the saviour".

She orders 12 women and children out onto the ice in temperatures of about 20 below zero. "Take off your clothes," she cries, "naked we must meet Jesus."

Before the night is over, four children and two women lay dead on the ice. Jesus does not come to rescue them.

All those involved are tried by a white man's court and sentenced to varying terms, except for Mina who undergoes psychiatric treatment.

The court orders that no further sporadic attempts at religious instruction be made and that the Inuit be left alone to their own religion.

CANADA'S PRESIDENT

We're having a wonderful time celebrating our 150th anniversary of Confederation this year, but did you know that it's 150 years since we elected our first and only president?

Yes, 1867 was a great year for Canada when we took that first giant step towards nationhood. But of course in 1867 Canada included only what are now the provinces of Ontario, Quebec, New Brunswick and Nova Scotia. The other provinces didn't become part of Canada until later. The last to join were Alberta in 1905 and Newfoundland in 1949. Until they agreed to become part of Canada those areas outside Confederation were still under the jurisdiction of the Imperial Government of Britain which in the Canadian West helped to create chaos.

In what are now Manitoba and the Northwest Territories, for example, the Hudson's Bay Company owned huge tracts of land, but did little to offer any kind of government. Thus, each individual settlement established some kind of unofficial council to administer such things as police, fire, roads, etc.

In the little town of Portage La Prairie, in what is now Manitoba, the local council was coming under increasing criticism for such things as too much drinking during meetings, so in 1867 local businessman Thomas Spence decides to take over not just Portage La Prairie, but the whole area.

Spence must have been a terrific salesman because he persuades many of the local residents to join him in petitioning the Imperial Government in London to form what he calls the Republic of New Caledonia which takes in territory now roughly within the boundaries of the Province of Manitoba.

Then, believe it or not, without waiting to get Government approval, Spence gets himself elected president of this new republic and begins levying taxes he says will be used for improvements. Everything goes along just fine until the Hudson's Bay Company, which owns most of the land, refuses to fork over a single cent of tax.

Then a local shoemaker by the name of MacPherson gets himself arrested on a charge of libel after publicly declaring that all the taxes collected are being used to buy liquor for Spence and his council.

MacPherson defends himself with so much vigour and evokes so much public sympathy that the Republic of New Caledonia collapses with Spence being tossed out of office.

Spence was hardly born under a lucky star since within two years he is editor of the newspaper called the "New Nation", the official voice of the next guy who tries to take over the place. A man hanged for his efforts—Louis Riel.

The next time you are in Winnipeg, take a stroll down Spence Street in recognition of the only president we ever had.

MONSTROUS FOLLY IN OTTAWA

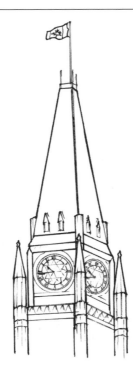

Canada's Parliament Buildings, to which hundreds of thousands will flock this year is called "a monstrous folly" by one of the Fathers of Confederation.

Worse, the Governor General of the day predicts that Ottawa wouldn't last four years as the capital of Canada.

The cornerstone of the new Parliament Buildings in Ottawa is laid by the Prince of Wales, later King Edward VII on September 1, 1860. Yes that's true—construction of the seat of our Federal Government begins seven years before Confederation. That is seven years before Canada is even a nation.

The appearance of such a grand building in the midst of what is a rough and rugged lumber town doesn't exactly thrill everyone.

The Honourable George Brown, the founder of the Liberal Party of Canada and a father of Confederation comes to town, looks around, shakes his head then writes to Sir John A. Macdonald.

"The buildings are magnificent, the style, the extent, the site, the workmanship are all surpassing fine. There is just one problem. They are just five hundred years in advance of the time. It will cost half the revenue of the province just to light and heat them and keep them clean. Such monstrous folly was never perpetrated in this world before."

Then as late as 1866, just a year before Confederation, Governor General Lord Monck writes,

"I am confident in my belief that notwithstanding the vast expense which has been incurred here in public buildings, Ottawa will not be the capital four years hence."

By no means is it the first or last time that politicians get something wrong.

All that remains of the original magnificent Centre Block and the Peace Tower is that large round building at the rear of the Centre Block. Only the National Library survived the devastating fire that destroyed the seat of government on February 3, 1916 taking the lives of seven people.

Both Brown and Monck were right about something. At last count the cost of renovations to Parliament Hill had reached 3 billion dollars with most of the work in the Centre Block's interior not scheduled to begin until 2018.

You can just imagine what either of them would have to say about more than three billion dollars for renovations when almost everyone back in those days was outraged when the full cost of building a railway from coast to coast in Canada reached an estimated $37 million.

A HAND IS SAVED

Everyone knows that Alexander Graham Bell invented the telephone, but did you know he once prevented a boy's hand from being amputated?

It is a few years before the launch of the 20th century, 1894, late October. The weather has been unseasonably cold, the swimming of summer is long over, the skating of winter not yet begun. One of the local women decides to hold a party for the restless boys of Baddeck, NS. There's a game of football, cake and cookies, but it's not quite enough excitement for eight year old John McCurdy.

"Let's have some fireworks," he shouts and leads a band of boys to the attic of his home where his father keeps a collection of guns. John picks the lock and soon they are removing gunpowder from bullets. They pour it out onto a newspaper, take it to a nearby yard and drop a match.

As McCurdy once told my father, "All we got was a poof of flame. I wanted something grander than that." He finds an old powder horn, fills it with gunpowder, holds it as far from his body as he can and drops a match into it.

The roar rattles windows a block away. At first everyone thinks John is dead. His eyebrows are gone, the right side of his face hardly recognizable. His right hand is little more than a gob of flesh.

Gangrene sets in. Doctors agree the only solution is amputation. They are about to begin the operation when Alexander Graham

Bell, a close friend of the McCurdy family enters, examines the hand and asks the doctors to wait another day. Respecting Bell's reputation they agree.

The hand is no worse the next day so they agree to wait another 24 hours.

Six months later John McCurdy has a new set of eyebrows, his face is as fresh as ever and he has regained full use of his right hand.

Fifteen years later, February 23, 1909, it is this same John Douglas McCurdy who makes history flying the Silver Dart, becoming the first man ever to fly in the British Empire and later becomes The Honourable J.A.D. McCurdy, Lieutenant Governor of Nova Scotia.

JUST A WORTHLESS TOY!

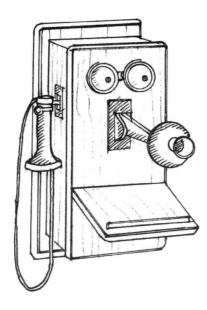

Alexander Graham Bell invented the telephone in Canada but for a time no one seems very excited. In fact when Bell offers to sell the patent for the phone to Western Union for $100,000, the president of the company turns him down flatly claiming, "The telephone is just a toy, not worth a thing." Two years later he sheepishly admits if he could buy the patent then for $25 million he would consider it a great deal!"

But Western Union isn't alone in those early days in disparaging this new invention. Less than a year after Bell makes his first and now famous long distance call (six miles) between Paris and Brantford Ontario, the Toronto Globe newspaper writes an editorial asking if the telephone is a failure. "It has serious problems" says the Globe "and is unlikely to prove very useful."

Totally unimpressed by the phone is the prime minister of the newly formed Dominion of Canada, Alexander Mackenzie. A private line is strung between Mackenzie's office on Parliament Hill and the office of Governor General Lord Dufferin at Rideau Hall. Even though the Government of Canada is billed only $42.50 per annum (payable in advance) the Prime Minister complains that it is so complicated and unreliable that he doesn't believe it's good value.

In fact he is so exasperated by this modernity that when his private secretary, during a test, becomes flustered and flubs his recitation of the Lord's Prayer, Mackenzie throws a minor tantrum and makes the poor man recite the prayer again.

The secretary had been sent to Rideau Hall to take part in a test of the connection. Hearing Mackenzie's voice coming from a wooden box fastened to the wall so excites him, William Buckingham completely forgets the words to the Lord's Prayer which is supposed to be part of the test call. The Prime Minister is not amused!

Even though Bell was granted the first patent for the telephone by the U.S. Patent Office and tells Canadian Parliamentarians that the invention occurred in Canada, many Americans have trouble admitting that one of the greatest inventions of mankind didn't occur on their soil.

So in 2002, believe it or not, the U.S. House of Representatives passes a resolution not only claiming that American Antonio Meucci is the true inventor of the phone, but that Alexander Graham Bell stole the idea from him!

It doesn't take long for the Canadian Parliament to respond to that outrage and only ten days later an all-party resolution is passed, declaring once and for all, that it was Bell who invented the telephone and furthermore he did it in Canada.

Nothing more was said. War was averted!

CRAZY LIKE A FOX

British Columbia once elected a premier who calls himself Amour de Cosmos which he explains means lover of the universe. Lover or not, he plays a major role in getting BC to join Canada and not the United States.

Few Canadians today realize how close BC came to joining the United States. There was even fear that the U.S. would simply annex the province to form a link with their newly acquired territory of Alaska. Joining the States would be very popular with the thousands of those lured west by the Yukon Gold Rush. In fact, at the time of Confederation 150 years ago, it's highly possible that the majority of residents in what is now British Columbia were Americans lured by the clarion cry of "there's gold in them thar hills!"

No one fights harder for the Canadian option than William Alexander Smith who, like so many young men, was lured from his home in Nova Scotia by wild tales of the Gold Rush.

Smith doesn't pan for gold but chooses instead to found the Victoria Colonist Newspaper at a time when, west of the Rockies, agitation is growing to join the United States. For some reason, perhaps to protect himself, perhaps just because he feels like it, Smith legally changes his name to Amour de Cosmos and sets out using his pen to promote the idea of joining Canada and not their burgeoning neighbour to the south.

His newspaper editorials are filled with vicious denunciations of local politicians who are opposed to joining Canada. Almost every edition of the Colonist is libelous by present day standards, but while no legal action is ever taken against him, hooligans often set upon him as he walks in the streets where his heavy cane is his sole defence.

But beaten and bloodied, as he often is, the next edition of his newspaper reports each fracas vividly, blow-by-blow with descriptions of "savage, beastly, human dregs employed by charlatan cringing, creeping politicians". That, by the way, is just one direct quote!

The pen finally triumphs and in 1871, British Columbia finally joins Canada. In the first election following its entry into Confederation, Amour de Cosmos runs in both the provincial and federal races and wins both! He sits, at the same time, in both the British Columbia Legislature and the House of Commons in Ottawa.

Less than a year later in 1872, Amour de Cosmos becomes British Columbia's first premier, resigning two years later to sit only in Ottawa.

Amour de Cosmos—described by one of the Fathers of Confederation as "a little crazy, but crazy like a fox".

Amour de Cosmos, lover of the universe, truly one of Canada's greatest, almost forgotten heroes! And characters!

THE HAT "TRICK"

It is an old felt hat that saves the life of the only white man to survive the infamous Frog Lake Massacre.

It is early spring 1885. Throughout the North West, Louis Riel is urging Indians and Metis to fight the Canadians. "Throw them off your lands," says Riel. "The Americans will come and pay you plenty of money for the land and then will trade with you."

Rebellion is in the air. Violence and murder break out.

Big Bear, Chief of the Cree who live along the North Saskatchewan River, is opposed to Riel, but his band members are angry and hungry. The buffalo, which for centuries have provided them with food and hides, are being wiped out; and the Cree don't think they are being treated fairly by Indian Agent Thomas Quinn at the Hudson's Bay outpost in the settlement of Frog Lake, now a part of Alberta.

Big Bear loses control of his people. War Chief Wandering Spirit takes over and attacks the small settlement at Frog Lake.

They capture all the whites at the Hudson's Bay Outpost, then in cold blood, murder them all except for two women and a trading post clerk named William Cameron. Among the nine dead are two priests and the hated Indian Agent Thomas Quinn who was the first to be shot.

Cameron, the young Hudson's Bay employee, was well liked by the local Indians and had made many friends, a fact which saves his life.

A few minutes before the massacre begins, an old man called Yellow Bear, warns Cameron to stay away from the other whites. Then when Wandering Spirit, in full war paint, orders Cameron to join the other men in the centre of the outpost, Yellow Bear objects claiming he wants Cameron to accompany him to the store to get an old felt hat he saw there earlier.

The store is only about 100 paces away but it saves Cameron's life. As he and Yellow Bear hide beneath some blankets, shots ring out only a few feet away and nine lie dead. Perhaps shocked at what they have done, the Indians spare Cameron plus two wives of traders and hold them captive for about two months.

Just prior to being hanged for his role in the massacre, Chief Wandering Spirit tells Cameron he had fully intended for him to die as well.

GET OUT OF CANADA

A single Canadian policeman accomplishes something General Custer and 700 of his cavalry troopers could not do, which is, get rid of Chief Sitting Bull.

Sitting Bull didn't actually take part in the Battle of Little Big Horn in which General George Custer and 274 of his men were killed. But he was the Chief and spiritual leader of the entire Lakota Sioux Tribe of the Dakotas that handed Custer his infamous defeat. As such, as you can imagine, Sitting Bull becomes a very wanted man in the United States, so the Chief and several hundred of his men flee north into the "Land of the Grandmother" as Canada is known to the Indians. The grandmother, of course is Queen Victoria.

The problem is, Canada is trying to convince people to settle the West. "Go West Young Man, Go West" is the advertising slogan of the day. All kinds of promises, including free land are made but with the infamous Chief Sitting Bull and his tribe roaming the prairies, getting young men and especially young women to move west is a mighty tough job indeed.

So tough a job, the call goes out for Canada's most famous policeman of the day, Inspector James Morrow Walsh.

"Get rid of Sitting Bull," is his order. "By the way we can't spare any men to help you." The Government of Canada expects one lonely North West Mounted Policeman to accomplish something that wiped out Custer and his men six years previous!

Walsh doesn't want any bloodshed so, with great courage and firmness, he manages to persuade Sitting Bull to leave, even though they all know American authorities will be waiting at the border.

The Chief spends two years in jail, then, incredibly becomes a featured attraction in Buffalo Bill's famous travelling show. He dies tragically when shot by an Indian policeman during a botched raid on a reserve in North Dakota.

Inspector Walsh goes on to become almost a legend. His mere presence is usually enough to prevent violence. He is called out of retirement upon discovery of gold in the Yukon in 1897 and as Chief Executive Officer in the Yukon, is able to prevent much of the violence and dishonesty that mark the Alaska Gold Rush.

Mount Walsh in the St. Elias Range in the Yukon is named after him and a memorial cairn has been erected in his honour in Fort Walsh, which he established.

THE POTATO ACCORD

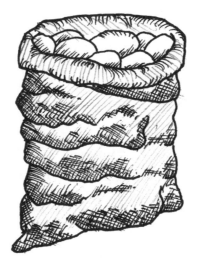

Have a look at the next bag of potatoes you buy. Chances are they represent an incredible story of survival and rescue that has a message for today.

Back in the early days of our history, just a few years after Confederation, Europeans aren't exactly beating down the doors to come to this cold, strange land with its wild animals and endless forests. So the New Brunswick Government, worried that French settlers will overtake the English, launch some vigorous recruiting. Fact is they lie mightily!

In so doing, they somehow manage to persuade a large group of Danes to immigrate to their province, promising them a wonderful new life with rich, cleared land and sufficient supplies to last that first winter.

But when the Danes arrive they find only dense forest, no cleared land and no supplies. Most of the immigrants are townspeople totally unprepared for agriculture or the vicious storms which soon lash the land.

Many of them, still dressed in top hats and clothes suitable for downtown Copenhagen begin to starve and freeze to death. The survivors travel up the Salmon River looking for some kind of settlement but find nothing. More than half of them die of cold and starvation.

The remainder are saved only when a group of French settlers stumble across the little Danish encampment. The French share what meagre supplies they have and from that precarious beginning, evolves what is one of the richest farming communities in all of Canada.

To this day that part of New Brunswick is called New Denmark and ships its famous potatoes to markets around the world.

The Danes never forget how the French saved them, and a number of years later, when the Roman Catholic Church burns to the ground, the Danes offer the use of their Lutheran Church and each morning, the emerging Catholics tip their hats to the entering Danish Lutherans.

The Catholics built their new church directly across the road from the Lutherans and this Sunday morning, indeed every Sunday morning, you will see Catholic and Lutheran greet each other with a smile and handshake and mingle on the road!

THE GHOST SHIP

Of all the mysteries of the sea there is none greater than that of the Mary Celeste, the "ghost ship".

She begins her career as the Amazon, built in the normal fashion of the day at Spencer's Island, Nova Scotia. The year of our Confederation, 150 years ago, she is driven ashore during a storm, later salvaged, modernized and renamed the Mary Celeste.

It's November 1872, the Mary Celeste leaves New York bound for Genoa, Italy with a cargo of raw alcohol. Nothing more is heard from her until December 5th when a British ship almost runs her through in heavy fog in the middle of the ocean.

She is abandoned. No sign of the crew or captain. No sign of a struggle. No signs of fire. She is still completely seaworthy with rigging intact.

The only things missing are the Captain's log and a lifeboat.

No sign of the crew or the lifeboat is ever found.

Stories of an attack by a giant squid or other sea monster begin flitting from port to port. Then word circulates that she is really a pirate ghost ship.

The Mary Celeste is towed into port, refitted for voyage once again but the owners have great difficulty in obtaining a crew. Most sailors consider her haunted, or at best jinxed, and refuse to go near her.

Investigations are launched. Rewards are offered for any information with knowledge of the ship or her crew.

But to this day what happened out there in the cold Atlantic remains a mystery.

Her career finally comes to an end during a storm in 1885 when she sinks off the south coast of Cuba.

THE SAVAGE'S WIG

When the Americans capture Toronto (yes they did!) they cart off a wig to show President Madison just how barbaric the Canadians really are!

It is actually the Speaker's wig taken from the legislative buildings but the invading Yanks think it's a scalp used in some kind of ancient rite by the semi-savages of the north. History doesn't record the president's response.

Actually Toronto is called York, Muddy York, by most during the war of 1812 and during the attack which occurred on April 27, 1813.

The invaders burn some public buildings, loot whatever they can find and just generally act like the victors they are. They occupy York for a couple weeks but their commander, General Dearborn, is having a devil of a time trying to make his way through the notoriously muddy streets of York. The General (after whom a city in Michigan is named) is so fat he has to be carted around in a special carriage which continually gets stuck in the mud. His soldiers are not amused!

This is the same Dearborn that couldn't quite make it to any of the fighting thanks to a bout of seasickness during the boat trip across Lake Ontario.

The attack is actually led by General Pike of Pike's Peak fame but Dearborn recovers just in time to lead a victory parade through the muddy streets of York, in his carriage of course.

The Canadians get their revenge about a year later when they attack Washington and set fire to what we all know today as the White House, then called the Presidential Mansion.

That's the reason it's called the White House. The fire the Canadians set scorches the building so badly that they try to cover up the damage with whitewash.

The American National Anthem's line "The rocket's red glare" of course refers to that attack. The anthem says "Our Flag was still there" and it was, but whatever happened to that captured wig we will never know!

THE COOK'S BEST FRIEND!

It is a wily Ottawan who cooks the world's first meal by electricity.

His name is Thomas Ahearn and while hardly anyone today knows anything about him he is undoubtedly one of the greatest inventors Canada has ever seen. His genius, according to those who have studied his feats, is comparable to those of Edison.

Ahearn starts his career as a telegraph operator and soon begins to show an amazing ability to invent electrical devices.

In 1882, just 15 years after Confederation, he establishes the firm of Ahearn and Soper, Electrical Engineers and Contractors, whose feats include erecting long distance telephone lines between Pembroke and Quebec City.

It's not long until his firm is given a charter by the City of Ottawa to build an electric street railway which when it begins operation in 1891 is the third such railway in all of North America.

Among his inventions is an electric sweeper to clear the snow in front of the streetcars which, as anyone who has lived in Ottawa knows, is a mighty good idea indeed!

But it's a year later that Thomas Ahearn comes up with the invention that should endear him to every cook for the rest of time - the electric stove.

It first goes on public display at the Ottawa Exhibition and wins a gold medal but to convince any doubters he agrees to actually cook a meal with his electrical apparatus.

Ottawa's Windsor Hotel is selected. Ahearn does the cooking himself, a full course meal, the first of its kind ever to be cooked by electrical power. From all reports, and there were many, the meal itself was quite good but the idea of cooking it by electricity said local newspapers was likely just a "passing fad"!

It was also Ahearn who in 1927, organized the broadcast of the Diamond Jubilee of Confederation, the first coast to coast broadcast in Canada.

Today, hardly anyone remembers Ahearn, there's virtually no recognition for him anywhere, not even on TV's MasterChef!

IT'S A DEAL

That store you love to shop in once sold 100,000 square miles of Canada for $2.50. That's right, two dollars and fifty cents for a big chunk of Canada.

Actually it wasn't your store that made the sale but rather the company that owns it, the oldest company in Canada, the Hudson's Bay Company, which before Confederation, owned most of Canada west and north of the Great Lakes.

The Company has a problem, because other than trading in furs it isn't doing much to promote settlement of the West and the British Government isn't very happy about it.

Afraid of losing some of its rights, the Company hands over a vast tract of land, actually more than 100,000 square miles for what amounts to two dollars and fifty cents to Lord Thomas Selkirk who has been successful in bringing colonists to Prince Edward Island.

The conditions of the sale are that Selkirk must bring at least 1,000 families to the territory he bought and he has only ten years in which to do it. A mighty tough job in those days.

Selkirk finds that no matter how poor their farms may be at home, most Scottish Highland peasants are reluctant to come to this new and strange land where wild Indians roam with the buffalo.

Selkirk offers all sorts of inducements, including a guarantee of free homes and 100 acres of land for every family that will head west.

Finally he manages to round up 105 men, women and children and in 1811 they set sail for Canada. It is a very hard voyage in a tiny storm-tossed ship.

They take the northern route to Canada through Hudson's Bay to the isolated fur trading depot of York Factory, a place so miserable that it was described by one fur trader as "a monstrous blot on a swampy spot with a partial view of the frozen sea".

That first winter spent in York Factory is one of the coldest in many years, but the hardy Scots survive and the following spring they set out south down the Red River until they reach the Assiniboine River, establishing a little settlement at what is now Winnipeg.

In fact their first buildings are erected at what is today "The Forks", Winnipeg's most famous site.

Thus it is that a small group of Scottish Highlanders, almost dragged from their homes by Lord Selkirk with promises of a paradise, are the founders of Winnipeg and become the first settlers to Canada's prairies on land bought for $2.50!

WORTHY OF A PICTURE

The next woman's face to appear on a Canadian twenty or fifty dollar bill (why not a hundred?) surely will be that of a little Irish woman known to her friends as "Little Sunshine".

Emily Murphy, what a woman! One of our country's great unsung heroes.

Born in Ontario, Emily moves west with her missionary husband around the turn of the 20th century. She is one of those people who does just about everything well.

Using the pen name Janey Canuck, she writes for the Winnipeg Tribune then authors a best-selling book.

She paints very well and wins awards for equestrian feats.

Her fame spreads when she organizes a group that pushes through the passage of the "Dower Act", which ensures, for the first time, that a widow receives at least a third of her husband's estate.

She campaigns for a children's protection act at a time when child labour is commonplace.

In 1916 she is appointed magistrate of a women's court in Edmonton, the first female magistrate in the British Empire.

Her work on the Bench provides insight into the problems of drug addiction and mental health. Her book "The Black Candle", addicts' name for the opium pipe, the first comprehensive study of the drug problem ever published in the world, is used extensively by the League of Nations as a textbook.

Emily campaigns for many years to have insanity recognized as an illness, not a crime as it was then.

In 1930 it is Emily Murphy who opens Alberta's first mental health clinic—one of the first in all of Canada.

But by far her most famous accomplishment is what becomes known as the "Persons Case".

Outraged that women are not allowed to become Senators, Emily Murphy, Irene Parlby, Nellie McClung, Louise McKinney and Henrietta Edwards petition the Supreme Court of Canada for a decision whether the British North America Act, which is our constitution at the time, allows women to become Senators.

On March 14, 1928 the Supreme Court rules that women are not "qualified persons" and thus cannot become Senators.

The fact that women are not considered persons is a bombshell throughout the Country. One woman writes: "The iron dropped into the souls of women in Canada when we heard that it took a man to decree that his mother was not a person!"

Undaunted, the "Famous Five" as Emily and her group become known, take the matter to the one authority even higher than the Supreme Court—the Privy Council in England.

On October 18, 1929, women around the world rejoice when the ruling comes down.

"Yes women are legally persons and thus can sit in the Canadian Senate." Lord Sankey of the Privy Council goes even further saying, "The exclusion of women from all public offices is a relic of days more barbarous than ours!"

Emily Murphy responds: "This decision marks the abolition of sex in politics. Personally I do not care whether or not women ever sit in the Senate, but we fought for the privilege for them to do so. We sought to establish the personal individuality of women and this decision is the announcement of our victory!"

Emily continues as a magistrate and juvenile court judge until her death four years later.

Her picture on new Canadian currency would be just one more accomplishment of a life filled with accomplishments! What do you think?

THE WATER SUPERHIGHWAY

The Rideau Canal, the oldest continuously operated canal system in North America is a pretty bucolic place today, but there was a time when it was a jam-packed superhighway.

Land along the St. Lawrence is becoming so scarce the United Empire Loyalists fleeing the American Revolution are forced to build their homesteads further inland. Confederation is still almost a 100 years into the future. There are nothing but Indian trails leading to the few settlements along the Rideau River.

Pioneers must carry supplies on their backs from the St. Lawrence River docks at Brockville and Prescott to their homes deep in the bush. Mosquitoes are so thick, one of Ottawa's founding settlers Bradish Billings, claims he was stung right through a large iron kettle he was carrying on his head! Women sleep in trees to avoid bears.

But when Colonel By completes the Rideau Canal in 1832 the entire area begins to thrive. The locks are jammed with boats, scows and timber rafts. The Rideau Canal becomes a 19th century superhighway. The steamboat called the "Bytown", chugs up and down the Canal carrying freight, animals, settlers and increasingly, tourists.

Within a few years there are hundreds of crafts along the Rideau: Steamboats, steam tugs, sailing scows, bateaux and log rafts with sails, bunks and cook houses. Each spring Indians in birch bark canoes haul furs to markets in Montreal. The most spectacular sights are the huge, noisy, smoky canal steamers, either side or stern-wheelers. Most of the paddlewheelers tow ten or

12 barges, often filled with travelling or holidaying people thanks to advertisements placed in newspapers as far away as Britain and France.

The hustle and bustle along the Canal is hard to imagine today. Barges unloading furniture, animals, luggage, mill equipment and people. All along the route steamers pull into wharves while a dozen or more men fill them up with cordwood.

By 1840, beautiful luxury liners are steaming the Rideau, featuring grand staterooms and carpeted dining salons.

The Rideau even boasts Canada's only recorded mutiny. A boat called the Enterprise springs a leak, then the engine breaks down. Those on board are short of provisions and during the night the cook mutinies, jumps overboard and swims away, never to be seen again.

Ah, those were the days!

FOX EYES

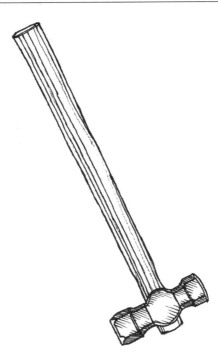

Fox eyes shining in the dark launch the world's biggest silver mine in Northern Ontario and a near riot on Wall Street! That's Fred Larose's story and he sticks to it till the day he dies.

Fred is working for the Ontario Northland Railway when it all starts. The track has reached a point about 120 kilometres north of North Bay when, according to him, he wakens in his tent and sees what he thinks are fox eyes shining in the dark. Fred says he throws a hammer at the fox and the next morning when he goes to retrieve it, he spots a chunk of rock the hammer chipped off. "I pick up the chunk and geeze there she is, a streak of pure silver," is what he tells a newspaper.

Fox eyes or not, it sets off one of the greatest mining stampedes in history. Within months more than 50 mines spring up. Thousands pour into the area. Claims are staked in every direction from the town of Cobalt which is the centre of it all. Other metals, including gold and cobalt are found. Kirkland Lake is formed, so is Porcupine. Noah Timmins and two others pay Larose $30,000 for his claim and the town of Timmins is founded. The population of Cobalt burgeons to more than 30,000.

Cobalt silver shares go on sale on New York's Wall Street creating such a near riot it requires mounted police to bring it under control.

Before it all ends ten years later, Cobalt mines produce 937 tons of silver worth in excess of $300 million (billions today). At its peak, Cobalt is the largest producer of silver in the world.

The Great Depression and WWII hit the area very hard between 1935-1946. All mines close. Cobalt becomes a ghost town.

But while there doesn't appear to be any silver left, today the demand for cobalt is picking up. Four mines are open. The boom is over but the population of Cobalt has grown to about 1,500 and since being designated Ontario's most historic town, some of the old mines are producing revenue again as tourist attractions.

THE GIANT

He's nearly eight feet tall, weighs an astonishing 580 pounds, wears a size 22 shoe, has hands almost a foot wide, and fatally injures himself lifting a 2,100 pound anchor.

His name is Angus MacAskill, the man known as the Cape Breton Giant. Even taking into account the fish story syndrome and local myths, there's no question he was one of the largest and strongest human beings who ever lived.

A kindly, gentle soul, Angus is the object of wonder wherever he goes. He can lift huge logs other men can't even move. One of his favourite tricks is to hitch himself to a plow and accomplish the work of a team of horses.

He becomes famous throughout the United States in the mid 1800's while being featured in a travelling show. The fact he is described as a handsome man with deep blue eyes and a deep musical voice makes him not only an oddity, but surprisingly attractive. He tours Europe for a time drawing huge crowds.

There is speculation that many of Angus's feats are mixed up with the legends concerning Paul Bunyan and vice versa, although the Cape Breton Giant certainly does not have a huge blue ox to accompany him. After making a small fortune with his side-show, Angus returns to Cape Breton and invests in several farms and a store. Locally he is known as Big Boy or "Gille Mor".

His death at a relatively early age is believed to have been the direct result of injuries he sustains while lifting a 2,100 pound ship's anchor to his shoulder.

When visiting Halifax be sure to see his life size statue at the Citadel Museum.

OF APPLES AND LOST LOVE

It's a tragic story of lost love that gives us our National Apple!

It's been 13 years since the American Revolution has ended but northern New York State is still in turmoil. Many of those who opposed the revolution and took the British side have already fled north into Canada as United Empire Loyalists. Others like the Irwin family which has settled in the fertile Mohawk Valley are refusing to leave despite constant harassment and threats.

But things change. A local farm boy, 18 year old John McIntosh, has fallen in love with the Irwin's 17 year old daughter Dolly. The teens want to marry but her parents are so opposed they decide to leave and join some of their former neighbours near Cornwall in Canada.

John is heartbroken, saves some money, and sets out to find his lost love. Finally he manages to track the Irwin Family down but is grief stricken to discover that his beloved Dolly has died.

Suspecting that the death may have been faked in order to persuade him to return home, John somehow arranges to have Dolly's body exhumed. Convinced of her death, (we don't know what caused her demise) John sets out on foot to find a farm as close as possible to her gravesite.

He settles on some scrub land in Glengarry County and as he clears the land for planting he discovers a few saplings growing wild. He knows they are apple trees but he's unclear on what kind.

Instead of plowing them under, John digs the largest sapling out and transplants it near his house. You probably know the rest of the story.

The little sapling grows into a beautiful large tree which produces big, red and delicious apples.

By this time John is married and has a son Allan who realizes the value of this wonderful new tree, grafts branches from it onto other apple trees, then creates a small nursery, continuing to experiment and improve the original stock.

Incredibly, that first tree produces fruit for 90 years finally dying in 1910.

Today orchards all over North America continue to produce juicy red McIntosh apples (the Mac) —Canada's National Apple and yes it's the apple that gave the Macintosh computers their name.

THE HATBAND MIRACLE

In far off Glasgow, Scotland a man dips his hat into a bin of strange coloured wheat. He's caught and ordered to dump the hatful back but a few grains are trapped under the hatband and a great Canadian industry is born!

We don't know the hat man's name, all we know is that he ships those few grains of wheat to his friend David Fife who is farming near Peterborough, Ontario and from that evolves the strain of wheat which creates the vast wheat fields of the Canadian West.

In the early days of Canada's development, a decade or two prior to Confederation, you just couldn't grow good wheat. The wheat brought to Canada from the British Isles and Europe was poorly suited to this country's soil and climate.

Farming when you had to root out primeval forests was almost impossible because all you had to plant were grains that usually froze solid before they had a chance to ripen. The grain which did grow was often of very poor quality.

One of those trying to develop a better type of wheat is David Fife, a young Scottish immigrant who has settled near Peterborough.

David writes a friend in Glasgow telling him of the problem. A few days after receiving the cry for help the friend learns of a shipment of especially good wheat which had just arrived from either Poland or Ukraine.

Down to the docks he goes and manages to steal a few grains of a reddish coloured wheat with his hatband and sends them to David.

David plants them all, but they produce only five stalks of fine quality wheat. Disaster strikes. Fife's cow gets loose and eats them all save one lonely stalk.

But that's enough. Fife plants the few grains left, selecting only the finest from each subsequent crop until he has developed the best, hardiest early maturing wheat in the world.

Unknown to his Scottish friend or to Fife himself, the grain captured in that hatband has a genetic component that allows it to adapt to diverse conditions. The wheat which Fife named Red Fife can grow hard or soft and be planted in either the fall or the spring. It adapts to warm or cold growing seasons, early or late springs.

It quickly spreads across Canada. Oceans of Red Fife wheat wave across the vast Canadian prairies. For decades it is our number one export product, feeding tens of millions of people around the world.

Gradually Red Fife is crossed with other hardy strains creating the Marquis Wheat which is the most popular variety grown today but every single stalk, every single grain owes its start to that one little stalk which survived a hatband rescue, an ocean voyage and a hungry cow's dinner!

WAR AVERTED

Believe it or not, a bank hold-up comes perilously close to plunging Canada into war with the United States!

The terrible American Civil War is almost over. Canadian Confederation is being seriously discussed, when somehow a group of about 25 soldiers from the almost defeated Confederate Army makes its way to Canada and sets up a base in St. John's, Quebec. It's not Washington or Abraham Lincoln they are after however, it's money!

It's October 19, 1864, a fine fall day. The Confederates sneak across the border and attack St. Albans, Vermont. Most of the town is burned to the ground, one Vermonter is killed and the banks are robbed of about $200,000.

With Union troops in hot pursuit the rebels flee back to Quebec and demand asylum.

The Americans are livid and demand the arrest of all 25. Rather reluctantly about half the raiders are caught and taken to Montreal for extradition hearings.

There's a day-long hearing but in the end the judge releases them and orders the stolen money, which had been confiscated, returned to them.

"This case is beyond my jurisdiction," explains the judge.

You can imagine the reaction from the Americans! Many of them, including leading politicians of the day, demand a declaration of war.

Speculation is that had the Civil War not already taken tens of thousands of lives and cost the U.S. treasury millions, war might have been declared. The fact Union troops are still fighting the Confederates across half the Country is also a deterrent.

But the denunciations from the Americans are loud and fierce. Canada is accused of supporting the Confederates, thus slavery! Individuals threaten reprisals.

Finally cooler heads on both sides prevail. Five of the raiders are re-arrested. The plundered banks are reimbursed their money and a note of condolence is sent to the relatives of the slain Vermonter.

But for a few days the fate of our fledgling Country is very much in doubt, providing a powerful motivator to get the Country out of the hands of the British who botched the whole thing very badly and to speed up the process of Confederation.

WHAT A WOMAN!

Winston Churchill may never have mentioned it, but some of the credit for victory in the Battle of Britain must go to a tiny, partially disabled Canadian woman, who surely must soon have a stamp in her honour.

Why more public recognition hasn't been given Elsie McGill isn't clear. For without the planes she built, it's doubtful that Britain could ever have withstood the onslaught of the German Luftwaffe.

Elsie was born a fighter. As a child, she suffered an attack of polio which left her severely handicapped but despite this she managed to successfully write her examinations in aeronautical engineering, becoming the first woman in the world to be qualified in the field.

Prior to WWII, she made a number of revolutionary aircraft design improvements while Assistant Chief Aeronautical Engineer at Fairchild's Aircraft. In 1938, with war looming, she is appointed Chief Engineer of Canada Car and Foundry in Fort William (now Thunder Bay).

She has hardly settled into her new position when the Department of National Defence hands her 3,600 blueprints and tells her to use them to build Hurricane fighter aircraft. It is an impossible task, at least for most. There are no skilled workmen to be found but Elsie, undaunted, brings in unskilled workmen, sailors, lumberjacks, farmers, women and in a short time teaches them to build airplanes.

Not just any airplane but the deadly Hurricane which becomes the mainstay of the fighter force defending Britain.

By 1940 Elsie McGill's plant is turning out more than 100 Hurricanes a month. She also perfects and builds 2,000 winterized Hurricanes with skis instead of wheels and somehow manages to design and build the Maple Leaf Trainor, the first airplane ever designed by a woman.

Many of the Helldivers used by the America Navy are turned out in Elsie's plant.

When Churchill makes his famous comment about so many owing so much to so few he is surely including Canada's Elsie McGill.

CANADIAN CAMELS

"I just shot the craziest lookin' bear ya ever seen," shouts Grizzly Morris to a group of fellow prospectors who flock to see. "That ain't no bear ya fool, that's my camel," cries one of them.

The Cariboo Gold Rush is on in earnest. Fortunes are being made—and lost. Billy Barker has a recurring dream of huge flakes of gold. He jumps ship in Victoria, travels up the Fraser River to a likely looking spot, stakes a claim, sinks a shaft and strikes gold to the tune of about five dollars a shovelful!

Barkerville becomes a rip-roaring town, attracting thousands from around the world. Tinkers, tailors, soldiers, sailors, ladies of the night, criminals, wise men and fools!

One of the craziest of all is a man named Frank Laumeister who, for some unexplained reason, becomes convinced he'll make a fortune renting camels as pack animals.

Somehow he manages to round up several of the humpbacks and ships them all the way up the Fraser Canyon north of Vancouver to the wilds of the Cariboo Mountains.

Needless to say it just isn't camel country and worse, they cause great consternation, especially when a prospector is suddenly confronted with one of them on the trail.

Grizzly Morris, who earned his name as much because of his appearance as his ability to hunt the big bears, meets face to face with a camel one afternoon on a bush trail. Convinced he's spotted the granddaddy of all grizzlies, he drops it with one shot between the eyes.

It is probably the most merciful death suffered by any of the poor animals.

We aren't sure exactly what happened to the others but they didn't last long in the bitter cold of the Coastal Mountains. While Frank Laumeister doesn't make his fortune, he certainly makes history as the only guy to ever try renting camels in Canada!

THE SILVER DART

Skaters bring the *Silver Dart* into take-off position at Baddeck on February 24, 1909.

Alexander Graham Bell is one of the few people present who anticipates the success of the Silver Dart, the first aeroplane ever to fly in the British Empire and Bell is the only one who immediately recognizes the historic significance.

It is February 23, 1909, the news that John McCurdy is going to try flying the Silver Dart over Cape Breton's Baddeck Bay spreads like wildfire throughout the community.

The entire countryside turns out to see the attempt as a one-horse sleigh tows the tiny plane out onto the ice.

McCurdy, wearing his favourite stocking cap, walks up to the machine, designed and built mostly by himself with Bell's assistance and guidance.

Finally the inventor of the telephone drives onto the ice. McCurdy tells him he's all set, ready to go, but Bell makes him wait until a doctor is present.

When local doctor Dan McDonald drives up, McCurdy clambers into the cockpit, someone cranks the propeller, the Silver Dart coughs to life, gathers speed along the ice and to the amazed gasps of the crowd slowly lifts into the air.

The Silver Dart climbs to a height of about 30 feet and flies for three quarters of a mile at about 40 miles per hour.

Since McCurdy intends this to be only a test run, he turns her around and makes a perfect landing as the crowd cheers and throws hats and mitts high into the air.

McCurdy tells Bell, ``She's all right now, I'm going to take her up for real." But Bell restrains him because he alone realizes the historical significance of the flight. He makes a little speech to the crowd saying that "what we have seen here may well prove to be one of the important pages in history".

Bell then announces that he has prepared a mammoth party with sandwiches, coffee and tea and the inevitable raspberry vinegar of which the amazing inventor is especially fond.

THE BARGAIN!

There`s only one way to describe it. The bargain of the century! How else would you describe paying only about $500 for downtown Ottawa including Parliament Hill?

Mind you, at the time Nicholas Sparks makes the deal, the Parliament Buildings don`t exist, nor do most of the buildings you will see today in Centretown Ottawa. It was the land he bought, bordered today roughly by Bronson Avenue to the west, the Rideau Canal to the east, Laurier Avenue to the south with the Ottawa River as the northern border—the heart of downtown Ottawa today.

It`s truly one of the great rags to riches stories in Canadian history because Sparks started his career as a humble farm labourer in Ireland and ended up as probably the richest man in Canada.

At this time, the ships carrying Irish immigrants to Canada are hell holes of filth, disease and despair. The death rate during some voyages is nearly 50 per cent.

Somehow, at the age of 23, Nicholas Sparks survives the horrors of the trip and gets a back-breaking job as a farm labourer in what is now the Hull portion of Gatineau. "Picking stones, yanking stumps and swatting flies," is how one historian describes it.

But he's a bright young man and sees opportunity. After nine years of hard labour, Sparks has somehow managed to save nearly 100 pounds. Just across the River from Hull he sees a vast tract of vacant land.

"I'll give you 95 pounds (about $500) for 200 acres of that land," he tells the owner. "Sold!"

He makes a profit selling bits of land almost from day one, but the really big money comes when Colonel By pushes his canal right through the centre of Sparks` property. Demand for land along the Canal skyrockets as Bytown grows in leaps and bounds but he really strikes it rich just after the Canal is completed. The government of the day seizes a big chunk of Sparks` property upon which they want to build a fort to protect the Canal. Sparks takes them to court and wins.

What a win! He is awarded a huge fortune of 27,000 pounds, worth millions in today`s currency.

As it turns out, Nicholas Sparks is a pretty good guy. He sits on the first elected council of Bytown and donates sites for the courthouse, the Carleton County Jail and the town`s first fire hall. In 1832 he donates the land upon which Christ Church Cathedral is erected, laying the cornerstone for that magnificent edifice himself on July 12, 1841.

Ottawa's pedestrian mall, Sparks Street, bears his name today.

ANOTHER SKYSCRAPER!

Is there something in the Nova Scotia water? Is it the air perhaps? Because not only is Nova Scotia the birthplace of the world's biggest man, the world's tallest woman hails from there as well.

Her name is Anna Swan, born in 1846 in New Annan, Nova Scotia, third child in a family of 13 and the only one of abnormal size.

By age 11, Anna is six feet one inch tall. Six years later at age 17 she has soared to seven and a half feet and by the time old P.T. Barnum of the Barnum and Bailey Circus finds her, Anna is eight feet, one inch tall, the largest woman in recorded history.

Barnum displays her at his famous New York Museum side-by-side with Commodore Nutt, the shortest man in the world. A favourite trick is to have Anna Swan balance Commodore Nutt on one of her fingers!

After the museum burns down, Anna returns to Nova Scotia but by now is famous.

She travels to England where the Queen, greatly intrigued, invites her to tea and presents her with a gold watch.

Shortly after Nova Scotia enters Confederation, Anna marries Captain Van Buren Bate, the Kentucky Giant who is one inch shorter than his bride.

The couple tours Europe and the United States for 14 months returning to the town of Seville, Ohio with a fortune.

They construct a huge house with 20 foot high ceilings and ten foot high doorways. As you can imagine, the house itself is a tremendous tourist attraction.

Tragedy strikes shortly after. Anna gives birth to two daughters both of whom weigh 20 pounds at birth and die in infancy.

Anna Swan, the most famous giantess in the world dies, in 1888 at the age of 42.

THE GREAT BLUENOSE
BOONDOGGLE

The original Bluenose, featured on our dimes, is the most famous ship ever built in Canada. The Bluenose II is our most infamous boondoggle. At least it would be if all the facts ever became public.

When that first Bluenose was launched March 26, 1921, construction costs, including rigging and sails were $35,000. When Bluenose II was finally finished being rebuilt in the summer of 2016 the cost had skyrocketed to $19 million with some repairs still required.

Where most of that money went we will never know. According to evidence at the famous "Gomery Inquiry", the Bluenose II rebuilding project was even dragged into Quebec's "Adscam Scandal". While most of the "Adscam" money ended up in Quebec pockets, somehow an estimated $2 million of federal money was sent to someone to help finance the ship's reconstruction but not a cent of that money ever showed up. At least not where it was supposed to.

There's no question that the Bluenose II is a beauty that very closely resembles the original but the man who captained the first Bluenose would be aghast at what happened to the second version.

Angus Walters, from all reports, was a very honest and extremely competent man who at the age of 30 built his own ship, then bought one of the largest vessels ever built in Nova Scotia. With this ship, the Gilbert B. Walters, Angus caught fish in numbers never again matched.

So it was only natural that the greatest skipper and the greatest ship of the day, the Bluenose would team up.

With Walters at the helm that first Bluenose won race after race. She was truly the "Queen of the North Atlantic", winning the International Sailing Championship five times.

Walters took the Bluenose to Chicago in 1933 to represent Canada at the Century of Progress Exhibition and four years later, sailed her across the Atlantic to take part in the Silver Jubilee of King George V and Queen Mary.

The Bluenose was the most famous sailing ship in the world!

Sadly, however, as steam replaced sails, the Bluenose was sold and was finally wrecked off the coast of Haiti in 1946.

A little bit of Canada went down with her.

Angus Walters wept!

A DEATHBED LETTER

A letter from a dying man launches the most incredible sea voyage in history.

Just as Canada enters the 20ᵗʰ century, John Claus Voss receives a mysterious letter from a man who claims to have discovered a huge fortune of gold nuggets on the Island of Cocos just off the coast of Costa Rica.

"I'm on board a ship returning from the Island right now," says the letter, "but I am dying so have given this letter to a friend to deliver to you!" The letter contains detailed instructions where to find the treasure worth $7 million!

Voss, a highly skilled small craft sailor and adventurer recruits a small crew, hires a small fishing schooner and sets out from Victoria, BC for Cocos Island and its hidden treasure.

On the way he encounters a very serious storm which sinks several much larger ships in the area. Voss manages to stay afloat and several weeks later reaches Cocos Island. Try as he might, Voss can't find the treasure but as he writes later, "The trip showed me that a small vessel is just as safe in a heavy gale as a large one and the idea to sail around the world in a small ship was born!"

And sail around the world he surely does, believe it or not, in a 32 foot long dug-out canoe fashioned from a giant redwood tree by a West Coast Indian.

On May 21, 1901 Voss sets out from Victoria headed westward. Most residents think the guy is nuts and don't believe they will ever see him again.

But, lo and behold, weeks later, Voss and the dug-out canoe he calls Tilikum arrive on the South Pacific Island of Suva. He doesn't stay there long before setting out again westward.

Voss loses his compass and most of his food in a vicious storm, but in an incredible feat he catches fish and laps up rainwater, floating all alone in that tiny canoe for more than a year.

The world believes him long ago dead when, about 13 months since Suva, he appears in Sydney, Australia. Now the world is fascinated but the spotlight doesn't suit John Claus Voss very well so incredibly, he sets out for South Africa.

He loses his way and months later sails back across the Atlantic to Brazil. He pushes off again, this time with a better compass and, believe it or not, three years, three months and 12 days since leaving Victoria, the Tilikum with Voss at the helm, sails into port at Margate, England.

The trip is at least 40,000 miles, probably much further.

Next time you're in Victoria stop by the Maritime Museum. There she is—all 32 feet of dug-out canoe—the Tilikum!

By the way, Cocos Island today is a Costa Rican National Park, a UNESCO Heritage site.

Did anyone ever find those gold nuggets? Ha, your guess is as good as mine!

THE MIRACLE OF THE BROTHERS

There are few happy endings to the grim story of the 1958 Springhill, Nova Scotia mine disaster, but none happier than that of the Hunter brothers.

When the deadly underground earthquake called a "bump" strikes Number Two coal mine on that tragic Thursday, October 23, 1958, Wilfred and Frank Hunter are working close together at the 1,300 foot level. Deep under the Atlantic Ocean!

When Wilfred comes to after being tossed about like a pebble in the bowels of the earth, his first thought is of his brother.

He calls out in the darkness but hears nothing, then groping about he feels a body, just above him pinned to the roof of the shaft. He is sure it is his brother.

For nearly seven days Wilfred lies there in total darkness with very little food and no water. All the while he is certain his dead brother is pinned just above him.

As the days drag on he becomes more and more convinced he will never again see the light of day, but a miracle happens. Rescuers poke through a metal pipe. Water and coffee are poured down and early the next day, Wilfred Hunter and 11 others are rescued.

Wilfred is in the Springhill Hospital when word flashes through town that more men have been found. Seven more as it turns out, rescued after eight and a half days buried in the mine.

Incredibly, one of those last seven is Wilfred's brother Frank. Wilfred doesn't believe it when I give him the good news until Fred is brought into the hospital and placed in the bed beside him.

There were many tears shed during those terrible days in Springhill, mine among them, but not all those tears were of sadness!

The rescues were heroic but in the end 75 men die in the Springhill Mine disaster. The mine is closed and Springhill ceases to be a mining town.

The Springhill Miners Museum, located only a few feet from where the Hunter brothers and all those rescued were brought to the surface is a major tourist attraction today.

One of the features of the Museum is a display of the rescue stories I wrote that were headlined in newspapers around the world.

THE BUNGLED BATTLE

One of the most famous, or perhaps infamous battles fought between Canada and the United States in the War of 1812 (mostly fought in 1813) was so badly bungled by both sides that no one ever wanted to admit they were there.

The Americans haven't had a whole lot of success invading Canada so in the fall of 1813 they decide to give it one final big push. Most of the attacks have occurred in what is now Ontario, but aside from setting fire to "Muddy York" (Toronto), British troops, local farmers and a few Indians have pretty well kept them at bay. So the Yanks decide to change tactics and attack Montreal, thinking that perhaps the French settlers might join them and revolt against the British yoke.

They assemble a large force of about 7,500 men along the northern border of New York State then, following the north shore of the Chateauguay River, start marching into Canada.

The British can only round up about 1,600 soldiers plus a few dozen Indians and a handful of settlers, so they dig in and defend a series of small gullies on the north side of the River near what is now Ormstown, QC.

The Americans think they can outsmart the British by simply crossing the River to the south side and skirt around the defences. It makes sense and infuriates the British who don't understand why the Americans don't attack them head on in the accepted battle fashion of the day.

But the Americans outsmart themselves. In crossing the River, many of them take a dunking in the frigid waters and foolishly light a series of campfires to dry themselves.

This, of course, lets the British and especially the Indians know exactly where they are. Most of the British refuse to leave their fortifications but a group of about 160, mostly French Canadians and Indians buck up their courage and strike out in the night through the woods and across the River towards the fires.

What follows next has never been made clear, mostly because no one, after it was over, would admit they were there.

There's lots of shooting, lots of shouting, lots of milling around in the darkness.

Five British are killed, several more Americans, but there's considerable evidence most, if not all, are shot accidentally by their own comrades.

What apparently happened is that the Americans became scattered in the woods and spent several hours shooting at each other—plenty of evidence as well that the Canadians did likewise. But it was the primitive war whoops from the Indians which finally convinced the Americans to pack it in and head back to the friendly hills of New York and Vermont.

It was a matter of great embarrassment to both sides, but in fact it was a victory for Canada, since the Americans never again tried to attack Montreal and shortly after, peace broke out.

There's an Historical Site to mark what is called the Battle of Chateauguay, but you will be hard pressed today to find someone admitting that anyone in their family tree was anywhere near the place when the shouting began!

UNDERTAKER SURPRISE

It is an undertaker who uncovers one of the most fantastic masquerades in Canadian history.

Doctor James Barry graduates in medicine from Edinburgh University in 1812, just as Canada and the United States go to war. Almost immediately the new doctor enters the British Army, rising rapidly in rank and is sent to serve in far flung outposts of the British Empire.

Although rather small in stature Doctor Barry is detested by colleagues, described as "an unsociable little beast," by many and has such a nasty temper is challenged to fight several duels, winning them all. The fate of the losers is unknown.

Although detested personally, the doctor is admired professionally as one of the best surgeons in the world, pioneering many innovations and procedures, some of which are today standard practice.

Doctor Barry comes to Canada as Inspector General of British Military Hospitals throughout the world and plays a major role in revolutionizing health care at a time when such things as hygiene and infection control are just becoming understood.

Just two years before Confederation, Doctor James Barry dies and while the body is being prepared for burial the undertaker makes a discovery that rocks much of the Western World.

Doctor James Barry is a woman who at one time gave birth! It is stunning news because in those days medicine is considered an immodest, if not immoral profession for women.

The discovery that one of the world's leading doctors is in fact a woman, shakes the profession to its very foundations, especially when rumours being floating around that the late Doctor Barry, whose real name was Miranda Barry, may have had a love affair with a member of the Royal Family.

But when the gossip dies down, the discovery that a female doctor could rise to a position of eminence in her field does much to lower the barriers against women entering the field of medicine.

THE PRANKSTER

One of the best things that ever happened to the field of medicine was William Osler getting expelled from school for unscrewing all the desks from his classroom floor and piling them in the attic.

Osler, who today is recognized as one of the greatest physicians of all time, was attending Trinity College Toronto in training for the clergy when he pulls one prank too many for the staid professors of the cloth. "Out you go", they order. Osler's mother is devastated. Osler not so much. He has something different in mind—medicine.

He enrolls in the Toronto School of Medicine and a world famous career is launched. While still in training, William Osler makes discoveries relating to the clotting of blood that earn him a professorship at McGill University at the age of 24. He immediately converts a cloakroom into a laboratory—McGill's first!

He revolutionizes the teaching of medicine, insisting that students, in addition to classroom work, see and work with patients and establishes the concept of medical residency. This idea that medical students actually work with patients, quickly spreads around the world and is standard procedure today.

New medical journals and societies seem to sprout everywhere he turns. He launches Canada's first meat inspection and writes no fewer than 1,200 books on medicine—one for every two weeks of his life.

He is a co-founder of the John Hopkins University School of Medicine, becomes the leading authority in the world on various kinds of heart disease, is the co-founder of the National Tuberculosis Association, and a pioneer advocate for better mental institutions.

In 1905 Osler becomes Regis Professor of Medicine at Oxford University in Britain and is made a baronet thus acquiring the title of Sir William Osler.

He leaves his extensive medical history library to McGill, including many rare books that have become the nucleus of one of the most important collections on medical history in North America.

Upon his death in 1919 the Times of London paid great tribute saying,

"His extraordinary influence was due partly to his great power of inspiring others, of getting the best out of his pupils and his high personal idealism. Many of the approaches to medical training he advocated, outlasted his considerable personal influence. Medical residency programs and a medical curriculum that includes bedside interaction with patients are still cornerstones of medical education today."

What the Times didn't say was that until the day he died, William Osler was not only one of the world's great physicians but one of its most famous pranksters. His little trick with the classroom desks was nothing compared to some of the other pranks he pulled. In fact, when news of his death was first published many of his friends didn't believe it thinking that it was just another of Osler's famous pranks!

THE PIANOMAN!

Try lifting a piano sometime. Now try carrying it over a snow covered mountain in the dead of winter.

Sounds impossible doesn't it? But one Canadian actually did exactly that—carry a piano over an Alaskan mountain!

Klondike Mike, born Michael Ambrose Mahoney near Buckingham, Quebec would probably make a fortune today playing professional football. Not only was he a tremendously powerful man with arms and neck the size of most men's thighs, but he was also quick and agile. Above all else he loved to fight. That is if he could find anyone to take him on!

Mike brawled his way through the American mid-west, often picking up beer and board money by performing feats of strength or taking on the local "tough guy".

But it isn't until the Yukon Gold Rush that Mike really finds his niche. He loves the north. The elements are far more formidable opponents than any man. For three years, Mike carries mail from Nome to steamboats along the Pacific coast. Tales of his strength and endurance spread.

Despite his prowess, however, there aren't many willing to bet with him the day he accomplishes the feat that makes him famous.

Incredibly, one day a piano arrives at the foot of the Chilkoot Pass, the most difficult portion of the 33 mile trail leading from Dyea, Alaska to Bennett Lake, BC.

Someone apparently wants to entertain the lonely prospectors of Dawson City which is just now springing up weed-like along the banks of the Yukon River.

One drink leads to another boast and before you know it, Klondike Mike finds himself in a big pickle! He either has to carry that piano over the pass or lose a good chunk of his pay.

The Chilkoot Pass boasts a 45 degree slope about three quarters of a mile up and a 45 degree slope three quarters of a mile down. Steps have been roughly chopped into the ice and snow. Just making it over the mountain unburdened requires tremendous strength and endurance.

With dozens of his drinking pals watching in amusement, with a mighty groan and heave, Mike hoists the piano onto his shoulders and begins the ascent.

He doesn't set it down again for two hours and a mile and a half up and down the infamous Chilkoot Pass. A prodigious effort never surpassed.

Eyewitnesses say the only feat to even approach it was the celebrating that followed.

Here's a little visitor alert. There's a little railway now that transports tourists over that famous Chilkoot Pass. Very interesting. What took miners most of a day to climb takes the train about 20 minutes. Good value, but that big bear you see as you climb then return. Not real. It looks real, the tourists "oh" and "ah" but I have news for you. It's stuffed!

HOBSON'S CHOICE

Freddie Hobson wins his Victoria Cross with a gun and a shovel, one of the most heroic acts of the First World War. It's an incredible story from an almost forgotten battle that took almost 4,000 Canadian lives.

The battle for Hill 70 in Northern France is almost as fierce as the one Canadians won a few weeks previous at Vimy Ridge about six kilometres away.

The Germans are determined to re-capture Hill 70 which overlooks the key city of Lens and for weeks, hurl themselves at the Canadian trenches in attack after attack.

On August 18, 1917, the Germans launch a heavy artillery barrage that smashes the headquarters of the 20th Canadian Battalion, blowing communication lines to pieces and greatly weakening the Canadian front. If they break through the front lines the Hill will be lost; hundreds, perhaps thousands of Canadians will die or be captured.

The weakest Canadian sector is known as Nabob Alley. There is only one machine gun left to stop the advancing Germans. Suddenly a shell plunges into the mud near the gun, burying both the weapon and the gunners.

Forty-one year old Sergeant Frederick Hobson, known to all his men as Freddie, dashes forward and with an entrenching tool, digs out one gunner who is still alive. Hurriedly they clear the gun and turn it towards the enemy, opening fire just as several Germans enter the trench. The muddy gun jams.

Freddie grabs his rifle and runs towards the advancing troops shouting, "Fix the gun, I'll hold them off".

With bayonet and clubbed rifle he bars the passage to the trench for several minutes. He's wounded several times but continues to fight. He hears a shout, "The gun is ready," but it's too late.

Freddie Hobson falls dead just as the machine gun rattles into action again, driving the enemy back, saving the sector and the lives of many men.

Freddie Hobson wins the highest award possible for bravery in battle—the Victoria Cross-- one of only 65 such honours awarded to the almost 620,000 Canadian men and women who took part in that terrible war that claimed almost 60,000 Canadian lives.

THE BEDPAN DECISION

A two week nursing career is enough to convince Florence Nightingale Graham to launch the world's most famous beauty aid company.

When Susan Graham gives birth to her first daughter just north of Toronto, not long before we enter the 20ᵗʰ century, Florence Nightingale is pioneering modern nursing and, aside from royalty, is the most famous woman in the world. It's not surprising then that the Grahams decide to name their firstborn Florence Nightingale Graham and are determined that she follow her namesake's career path.

From earliest childhood Florence is encouraged to enter nursing. At every opportunity Florence Nightingale's ground breaking accomplishments in improving hospital conditions are discussed and praised.

Florence herself isn't totally convinced that nursing is what she wants to do, but she enters nursing school, graduates and signs on with a local hospital.

She lasts exactly two weeks.

"That was enough," she later tells reporters, "two weeks of emptying bedpans convinced me I needed to do something a bit more glamorous".

Does she ever!

At that time, cosmetics are virtually unknown and indeed in many circles are considered quite sinful. Women usually resort to pinching their cheeks to give them a bit of colour.

Florence heads out for the big city, New York, and goes to work for a chemist who is developing a face cream. She learns everything she can from him, then with $600 of borrowed money, she opens the world's first beauty salon, right there in the heart of New York, on Fifth Avenue.

It is the first of millions of such salons all around the world, many of them owned by Florence Elizabeth Nightingale Graham who becomes the richest woman in the world.

You'll probably recognize her name and her products if I tell you the name she assumed in order to escape all the jokes about nursing, Elizabeth Arden.

THE GODS ARE FROZEN!

Trial marriage is nothing new. The Huron Indians of Ontario were giving it a fling when Columbus sailed his "ocean blue".

It was actually Champlain who made the discovery. He helps the Huron Indians attack the Iroquois at Lake Onondaga in the fall of 1615. The Hurons are defeated and Champlain is badly wounded, forcing him to spend the winter in a Huron village near what is now Orillia, Ontario.

Champlain wishes dearly he'd left the Indian wars alone, but it does provide him with an excellent opportunity to learn many native customs and beliefs.

The Indians are afraid to discuss their gods and folklore during the summer because they believe the gods perch on their shoulders and hear everything they say. During winter however, the gods are frozen in the ice and so they talk freely.

The Hurons tell Champlain that their young women live freely with several men until an agreement is reached to form a permanent partnership with one of them.

To seal the agreement, the husband gives her gifts of wampum (jewelry made of multi-coloured shells) and skin belts.

Champlain also learns that the Hurons have many beliefs very similar to those of the Christian faith.

For example, one of their versions of creation is similar to the biblical rendering in Genesis.

A translation means, "At first there were great waters above the land and above the waters were thick clouds and there was god the creator".

Champlain's findings are very enlightening but sadly his taking sides with the Hurons turns the Iroquois against the French, costing many lives, French and Indian, in the decades following.

Disease and tribal warfare decimate the Huron population, virtually wiping the tribe off the face of the earth.

THE CHICKEN GAME

Back in the good old days of a six team National Hockey League, the Montreal Canadiens always played the Toronto Maple Leafs in Toronto during the Royal Winter Fair, strictly because of the chickens.

Frank Selke Senior, General Manager of the Montreal Forum and the Canadiens along with Dick Irvin, the "Silver Fox", Coach of Les Canadiens were chicken buffs. Between them they raised some of the finest exotic chickens in the world and as Toronto's Royal Winter Fair was one of the finest agricultural fairs in the world, it was only natural that Selke and Irvin would have a good many of their prize chickens on display there.

So keen were they to follow the fortunes of their fancy birds that every year, these two "Hockey Hall of Fame" recipients made sure the Canadiens were booked into Maple Leaf Gardens during poultry judging day at the "Royal".

It required some co-operation from the other teams, of course, but in those pre-television days it posed no real problem.

So bright and early comes the day their chickens are to be judged, Selke and Irvin, two of the most powerful and influential men in hockey, anxiously follow the judges from cage to cage, rejoicing or sorrowing just as much at the victories or losses of their chickens as they will that evening when their hockey team takes to the ice against the Maple Leafs!

Both Frank Selke and Dick Irvin lived in Upper Westmount, on the side of Mount Royal. Selke's chickens were housed on my father's farm about 20 miles north, but incredibly, Irvin was allowed to erect a number of small coops around the mountainside with his chickens free to graze the grass that grew wild.

When Irvin left the Canadiens to coach Chicago, the job of rounding up his chickens fell to me. The wily birds had no desire to leave Canada, with the resulting wild chase along the mountainside providing considerable amusement for some of Canada's more affluent citizens watching the show from their backyards. None of whom, let me add, offered to help!

CANADA 150

THUMBS DOWN
TO TORONTO!

The pretty little town of Port Hope could have been given the name Toronto, but the residents turned it down as a really dumb name!

Port Hope is a picturesque small town on the north bank of Lake Ontario, well known today as having the best preserved 19th century streetscape in Ontario. It began as a Cayuga Indian village called, of all things, Ganarski. Later, when a trading post was established there by Peter Smith, it appropriately enough was called Smith's Creek, settled almost entirely by United Empire Loyalists fleeing the United States after supporting the British in the Revolutionary War.

The War of 1812 between Canada and the United States leaves the little village badly shaken. With the Americans just on the other side of Lake Ontario the Loyalists decide they need more British subjects in town to better defend themselves. Someone suggests in order to attract more British settlers they need a name that sounds a bit more encouraging and modern than Smith's Creek.

For some reason the name Toronto had come into general use in the area about 60 miles (100 kilometres) east of the town of York which, of course, years later, did assume the name Toronto. When a post office is established in Smith's Creek, officials tell the residents they must make up their minds and decide what they want to name the place.

A public meeting is held during which several names are kicked around, including Toronto, which is turned down in a recorded vote. "Toronto is a terrible name," is the consensus, "it doesn't mean anything and sounds dumb when rolling off the tongue." Or words to that effect!

Then someone suggests Port Hope. "We want something inspirational, something that will attract new settlers," says someone, "Port Hope is perfect." Everyone likes it and with surprisingly little opposition the name Port Hope is officially adopted.

It isn't quite clear why the name was proposed but was undoubtedly in honour of Colonel Henry Hope, Lieutenant Governor of Canada a few years previous and a great friend of the United Empire Loyalists fleeing the United States.

The community westward up the Lake apparently wasn't as fussy about its choice of names, because about 15 years after Port Hope turns thumbs down on the name, York, usually called Muddy York, is incorporated as the City of Toronto.

To this day, residents of Port Hope will tell you they got the better of the deal and not necessarily just as it relates to the name either!

TORONTO THE POLLUTED?

Do we have pollution to thank for giving Toronto its name? Many historians believe so.

The word "Toronto" is believed by nearly all authorities of such things to be of Iroquois origin, but as frequently occurs, agreement ends there.

A leading U.S. Indian authority says the Iroquois word "thoron-to-hen" means timber or fallen trees in the water. Another student of the Iroquois traces Toronto to "de-on-do" which he translates into, "logs floating on the water".

Thus, it would appear that the floating debris in what is now the City of Toronto Harbour was significant enough, even before the white man arrives, to be noteworthy.

Some theories say the word isn't from the Iroquois language at all, but is actually derived from the Huron for a place of plenty, either ducks, fish or people.

Toronto, of course, actually got its start as the Village of York, in honour of the second son of King George III. It wasn't long until it was far better known throughout the length and breadth of Upper Canada (Ontario) as Muddy York, in recognition of the goo which covered everything from thaw to freeze up.

It was incorporated as a city in 1834 and has since been called Toronto the Good, Cabbage Town and a few other names not suitable for family reading!

Named the capital of the newly designated province of Ontario at the time of Confederation, Toronto today is the fourth largest city in North America. Only Mexico City, New York City and Los Angles have greater populations.

PICTURE PERFECT!

Very few history books acknowledge this fact, but it's highly probable that a painting had more to do with selecting Ottawa as Canada's Capital than the threat of American invasion.

Most school children today are taught that Ottawa was chosen as our Capital as a compromise between the claims of Montreal and Toronto and because of the fear of invasion from the United States. For a time, even the city of Kingston was in the running to be the seat of government, but it, as with both Montreal and Toronto was considered by some, too close to the American border to be safe from attack during those tense early days following the American Revolution.

But in fact, probably a painting done by Lady Head, the wife of Governor General Sir Francis Bond Head, decided it.

Lady Head visited Ottawa and was charmed by its setting overlooking the Ottawa, Gatineau and Rideau Rivers.

An accomplished painter, Lady Head completed a beautiful water colour of Major's Hill, overlooking the Ottawa River close to what is now Parliament Hill.

Back in Britain a short time later, she showed the picture to Queen Victoria who was having a difficult time making up her mind where to locate the capital of this burgeoning new country.

According to several accounts, the Queen was delighted with the picture and exclaimed, "That is the place."

The die was cast!

Thus, despite the advice of almost everyone who knew anything about Canada, Ottawa, a small, rough and tough lumbering town at the time, was named the seat of government in 1857—ten years before Confederation. And the rest, as they say, is history.

NO TEXTING!

Not only is there no texting among Old Order Mennonite teenagers, there's no television or radio either which adds to the mystery of how the Mennonites of Southwestern Ontario are able to keep so many of their children from wandering away to a more modern life.

Childhood for young Mennonite children is usually a very carefree and fun filled existence, even though they don't have any of the modern toys that seem to fill the bedrooms of most North American children.

The little Mennonite girl may have a few rag dolls, the little boy will likely have a hand-made wagon or buggy. From a very early age they will interact freely with the farm animals and anyone who visits a Mennonite farm or home can easily see the children, especially the young ones, are bubbling with happiness. It is, after all, a very safe and secure home for most of them.

When the children grow a little older, life isn't quite as carefree. When the Mennonite girl reaches the age of 14 or 15 she'll replace her child's pinafore with a cape and apron. Her skirts will become longer and she'll start fixing her hair into a bun.

The teenaged girl will work on her father's farm. Up at six or earlier in the morning to help with the milking, then household chores, washing, ironing, cooking and mending. During summer afternoons she will be outside hoeing or weeding the garden.

The young man's day starts at the same time and he works just as hard in the barns and fields.

Sunday though, is a day of rest, socializing and for the older teens, a day of courting. It's up early; harness a horse to a well-polished black buggy and off to church whose parking lot will soon be filled, not with cars and trucks, but horses and buggies. Sunday afternoons are then spent visiting and entertaining friends, Sunday evenings are for the young people.

Teens of courting age will probably spend Sunday evenings in a friend's home, talking or singing hymns. Some of the more modern young people may even do a bit of square-dancing, but that's not totally approved by older members.

It all sounds like a life filled with drudgery but even those who do find the life too stifling and leave the Order will tell you that they recall their childhood and youth as a very exciting and fulfilling time.

Very few actually do leave the Order or express any desire to do so despite all the modern inducements.

Juvenile delinquency, unemployment, drug or alcohol abuse, welfare? Those are words most Mennonites don't even understand!

SHOOTING STAR

That's a magnificent monument we have built to General Brock at Queenston Heights. The red coat Brock was wearing when he was shot dead defending Canada against the Americans is on display at the National War Museum in Ottawa. The hole from the bullet which killed him can plainly be seen, but it was an Indian Chief as much as Brock, who saved Canada during the War of 1812.

Shooting Star was his name but he became much better known as Tecumseh. Brigadier General Tecumseh, as a matter of fact, something many of our history books don't tell us.

He is born a son of a Shawnee Chief at a time when Indians roamed freely throughout what is now the State of Ohio. As the white man moves westward, disregarding various treaties, Tecumseh organizes a union of several tribes which fight the encroaching Americans who seem determined to wipe out native populations entirely.

But after several defeats, Tecumseh realizes the only chance his people have of staying alive is to join the Canadians (the British) in their fight against the United States in the War of 1812.

Several thousand of his warriors join him as he crosses Lake Erie and joins the "Red Coats", providing them with what most historians now agree, are their best fighting men.

Tecumseh was a brilliant tactician. He showed Brock the best way to invade Fort Detroit and in fact Tecumseh's men had the Fort convinced to surrender without a shot being fired. There is plenty of evidence that if Brock had followed Tecumseh's advice, most of the state of Michigan would likely be part of Canada today. The deal with Tecumseh was that if the Canadians could beat the Americans and hold Fort Detroit, most of what is now Michigan would be deeded to the Indians.

The great chief, now a Brigadier General, and his men fight bravely in several other battles and while Tecumseh is dead by this time, his men try to rescue Brock as he lies dying during the Battle of Queenston Heights.

During that fierce battle, these same warriors play a major role in driving the Americans back across the border, even as Brock is dead, thus in all probability avoiding a defeat which would likely have spelled the end of Canada as we know it today.

Tecumseh is killed while fighting invading Americans at Moraviantown near Chatham. His body is carried into the deep woods by his warriors and all trace of him is lost forever.

Brock, his great friend, who rode side by side with him during the capture of Detroit, describes the Chief as well as anyone could when he said of Tecumseh, "A more gallant warrior does not I believe exist."

CANADA 150

THE FOOLISH
AND THE WISE

You can still see the bullet pockmarks on that historic old windmill near Prescott, Ontario, but what most don't know is that those bullets helped launch the political career of our first prime minister.

It's a crazy story in a way but back in the days just prior to Confederation, a secret society springs up in the United States with the goal of invading Canada and forcing us to become Americans.

Called the Patriot Hunters, or just the Hunters, at one point they claim to have 150,000 members who believe that capturing Canada would be very easy with most Canadians joining them in booting out the British authorities.

The St. Lawrence River at Prescott is very narrow so the Hunters say, "Let's attack there, we'll catch them by surprise." Since some of the Hunters were known to boast a bit when drunk and there was plenty of drinking and boasting, the Canadians were completely aware of what was happening.

The whole thing is a major screw up. A couple of the attack boats hit a sandbar, another gets lost. The leaders decide to head back to the States, they claim, to get reinforcements—but a group of about 200 makes it to a large stone gristmill at what is now called The National Battle of the Windmill Historic Site near Prescott.

For five days they hold off attacks from about 600 militiamen but when the navy shows up, with large guns trained on them, the Patriot Hunters give up. Eighteen of them were killed in the siege, the rest are arrested and hauled off to Kingston for trial.

Since their leaders deserted them, the Windmill defendants chose a poor man named Nils von Schoultz to lead them.

As luck would have it, a bright young Kingston lawyer by the name of John Macdonald agrees to represent von Schoultz.

Even though Macdonald loses the case with his client sentenced to death, the young lawyer's courage in taking the case and fighting so hard for an unpopular cause wins him the admiration of Kingston and his political career is launched.

The case does something else for Macdonald. It convinces him that Canada must be united to resist the pressures of her powerful neighbour to the south, a belief that leads him to spearhead the creation of the Dominion of Canada and become our first prime minister, the "father" of our country.

THE PATRIOT HUNTERS

Despite the disaster of the "Battle of the Windmill" during which more than 200 of their members were either killed, deported, jailed or hanged, the mysterious Patriot Hunters Society continues planning to attack and capture Canada.

Hunters' lodges spring up in northern Vermont, New York State and Ohio. More than 150,000 take the secret oath of allegiance. There have already been several armed rebellions against the British administration in Canada and the Hunters believe they can launch a successful, American style uprising of the Canadian population against British rule, with a properly carried out invasion.

They fail badly at Prescott during the Battle of the Windmill, they fail again in an attack near Windsor, but it seems to only make them more determined.

More secrecy is needed they believe, so elaborate signs and passwords are devised for recognition within the Patriot Hunters membership.

The snowshoes are soldiers without rank, beavers are commissioned officers, grand hunters are field officers, and the Patriot Hunters become the highest ranks.

All recruits are required to take an oath while blindfolded stating. "I solemnly swear in the presence of Almighty God, that I will not reveal the secret signs of the snowshoes to any, not even to members of the Society. I will not write, print, mark, engrave, scratch, chalk or in any conceivable manner make the shape or sign of the snowshoe to any living being, not even to members of the Society."

The oath went on at some length promising that the new member would not reveal any plots against the Society.

Once the oath is given, the blindfold is removed to reveal a burning candle, a naked sword pointed at the recruit's heart and two pistols flashed in his face. He is then promised that his throat will be cut should he in any way fail to live up to his oath!

Despite all the oaths and secrecy the Patriot Hunters fail in their attempts to capture Canada, in fact just the opposite happens. The constant threats from Americans have a unifying effect on Canadians and in no small way convince us to speed up the process of Confederation.

ACE

Thousands of people are praying for the recovery of one of hockey's greatest stars. Radio stations in the United States and Canada broadcast hourly bulletins on his condition. A doctor gives him only hours to live. A little nurse spends a night slapping his face to keep him alive, then yet another crisis, solved by a chicken fancier.

Ace Bailey, star forward with the Toronto Maple Leafs hovers near death in a Boston hospital, having been checked to the ice a few days before by Eddie Shore in the Boston Gardens.

Radio stations are urging everyone to pray for his recovery, but there is little hope.

Plans are made to ship his body back to Canada. At his bedside is a little nurse, recalled by those who were there only as Miss Ahn. Whenever Ace seems to be slipping away she slaps his face gently and says, "Ace, keep fighting, your team needs you!"

Then in the midst of the crisis, Maple Leaf Team Assistant General Manager Frank Selke gets a phone call in Toronto. Team owner Conn Smythe is on the line. There's another emergency. Ace Bailey's father is in a Boston hotel room. He's got a gun and swears he's going to kill Shore.

"Do something and do it quick," orders Smythe.

Selke begins to tick off the names of everyone he knows in Boston, then recalls a fellow by the name of Bob Huddy, a Boston policeman who, like Selke, raises and shows fancy chickens.

'Sure," says Huddy. "Glad to help out."

Huddy finds Mr. Bailey, talks him out of the gun, puts him on a train and orders the conductor not to let him off before Toronto.

Incredibly, Ace Bailey survives. He never plays again, but is there to shake Eddie Shore's hand during the Ace Bailey Benefit Game February 14, 1934 the first All Star Game in NHL history.

For the record, the Maple Leafs won that first game, defeating a team of All Stars from the five other clubs 7-3 before a crowd of 14,074 cheering spectators.

CANADA 150

9/11 AND THE STANLEY CUP

September 11, 2012, the Stanley Cup is gently placed on top of Panel S-3 at the South Pool of the September 11 Memorial in the heart of New York City.

There are few dry eyes among those in attendance, including members of the Los Angeles Kings who won the Cup that spring. As the trophy comes to rest directly over the names of two of the victims of the deadly 9/11 attacks, heads bow in prayer and remembrance of Garnet "Ace" Bailey and Mark Bavis.

Bailey, the Chief Scout for the Kings and Bavis, an amateur player scout, also for the Kings were aboard United Airlines Flight 175 when it was hijacked by Islamist terrorists who crashed it into the south towers of the World Trade Center on September 11, 2001.

Both were travelling from Boston to Los Angeles after visiting Manchester, New Hampshire where they had recently placed an AHL team called the Monarchs.

Their names are memorialized on Panel S-3 of the National September 11 Memorial along with all 2,606 victims of the Twin Towers attack.

The idea to bring the Stanley Cup to the Memorial was that of Kings General Manager Dean Lombardi who was there at the special ceremony, along with many other team officials and players, to pay tribute to their fallen comrades and so that in Lombardi's words, "the families of both Bailey and Bavis would have their day with the Cup."

It seemed especially fitting in that the Canadian born Bailey's name (no relation to Ace Bailey of the 1933 Leafs) is inscribed four times on that Stanley Cup—twice as a player with Boston, twice as a leading scorer with Edmonton.

REMNANTS OF THE PERFECT STORM

If you saw the movie The Perfect Storm, or read the book, you know the tragic fate of the Andrea Gail and her crew. What you may not know is that the only traces of that ill- fated ship after she went down, washed up on the shore of Canada's "island of the wild ponies".

Nine days after the Andrea Gail's last radio transmission, the emergency positioning indicator, a fuel drum and an empty life boat from the sunken ship floated onto the sandy banks of Sable Island about 300 km (190 miles) southeast of Halifax. They are the only traces ever found of the 72 foot fishing vessel and her six-man crew.

Her last reported position was 290 km (180 miles) north east of Sable Island on October 28, 1991. At about 6 p.m. Captain Billy Tyne broadcast his co-ordinates and reported rising seas. His final recorded words were, "She's comin' on boys and she's comin' on strong!"

It is ironic that historic Sable Island with its famous wild ponies would receive the final traces of the "Perfect Storm" tragedy since this is the island that for generations was known as the "Graveyard of the Atlantic".

Amazingly, before two lighthouses were erected immediately after Confederation, there were no fewer than 350 shipwrecks that either washed ashore on Sable Island or ran aground on her sandbars. At one time, 50 people were stranded on the Island for five years with only 11 surviving. Many of these wrecks are still there, buried beneath the ever shifting sands.

The wrecks share the Island with about 400 wild ponies whose ancestors were probably victims of one of those shipwrecks. The ponies and Island are now protected by the Nova Scotia Government which severely limits access to only a few hundred people a year.

What isn't widely known is that Sable Island is gradually shrinking, as the sand is slowly washed away by the Atlantic tides.

Each one hundred years the Island is reduced in size by about one quarter which means that Sable Island will likely disappear completely in a couple hundred years or so.

THE SLAVE

One of the greatest cowboys and finest gentlemen who ever rode the Western Range was a former slave!

John Ware is freed from slavery by the Union Army near the end of the American Civil War. He immediately leaves his home in South Carolina and heads to Texas.

There, his talent for handling horses and his ability to make friends gradually wins him recognition as one of the Southwest's best cowboys.

Eventually John moves northward with various cattle drives until shortly after Confederation, he comes to Alberta's High River district where he falls in love with Canada.

When the trail riders are paid off and head back to the United States, John stays on at the "Bar U Ranch" as a hired hand. No one is better with horses than this huge black man. He can break the meanest bronc. That isn't his only skill.

He begins wrestling steers ten years before "bulldogging" is invented by another former slave cowboy—Will Pickett. While an excellent shot with a six-gun and rifle, John never uses them against his fellow man. His honesty is widely recognized and his strength becomes legendary. In a country where heavy drinking and rowdiness are the rule, he remains sober and dependable.

It isn't long until John is appointed foreman of the "High River Horse Ranch", then a few years later he buys a ranch of his own and by the turn of the century has one of the largest cattle herds in Alberta.

He marries a Calgary woman, has five children then in 1905 is killed when his little cowpony steps in a badger hole and rolls on top of him.

John Ware is buried in Calgary where thousands turn out to pay tribute.

Songs have been written about him, a Calgary high school bears his name as does a college building; and just a few years ago the log cabin in which he lived for a while was moved to the Dinosaur Provincial Park at Drumheller, AB as one of its key attractions.

A tribute to a mighty man and a tribute as well to our great Canada.

IRISH FOLLY

A harebrained scheme to capture Canada and hold her ransom in exchange for Irish independence is the final straw convincing doubters that Confederation is the only thing that can save us from constant American invasion.

First it was the crazy Patriot Hunters who attacked us near Prescott and Windsor in the mistaken belief that Canadians would join them in overthrowing British rule.

No sooner did we give the Hunters the old heave ho, then lo and behold a group of Irish begin eyeing Canada as an easily captured pawn in the deadly civil war being waged in Ireland.

The Fenian Brotherhood is organized in New York City in the mid 19th century to assist the Irish rebels, who were trying to throw the British out of Ireland. No one pays them much attention until thousands of Irish men and women flee their homes for the United States and Canada when the British crush the uprising.

Somehow a plan is hatched by the Fenians to invade and capture Canada. This, they believe, will serve two purposes: Drain away British troops from Ireland and hold Canada as ransom for the freedom of their homeland.

The plan is that four forces will enter Canada just one year before Confederation. One of the attacks is to be at Fort Erie, another at Prescott with the troops there to strike directly towards Ottawa where the Parliament buildings are awaiting the new Government of Canada. A third attack is planned to head for Montreal through the Eastern Townships of Quebec, and the fourth attack is to capture Campobello Island just off the New Brunswick shore.

The only attack with any success for the Fenians is the "Battle of Ridgeway" near Fort Erie where a group of about 700 overwhelm a small group of Canadian volunteers. When reinforcements arrive, the attackers flee back to the United States. No other attack is successful but they do accomplish something.

A group of about 750 Fenians assemble on the Maine Coast opposite Campobello Island but quickly disperse when British warships show up with cannons at the ready.

At the time there is strong opposition in New Brunswick to the idea of joining with Quebec, Ontario and Nova Scotia to form The Dominion of Canada, but the threat of being left alone to fend for themselves in the event of another invasion is sufficient to persuade all but the most diehard objector to become one of the four founding provinces of Confederation.

AN APPLE AND A SMILE

One of the largest supermarket chains in the world is started by a plucky little Montreal woman with $300 and a big smile.

It's a year before the end of the First World War when Ida Steinberg invests her life savings of $300 into a small grocery store in downtown Montreal.

Competition is stiff, especially for a Jewish woman trying it on her own, but Mrs. Steinberg uses a secret to turn her little store into a giant among giants.

She makes a point of getting to know every one of her customers by their first name, greets each one with a big smile when they enter and often tucks a free apple into their shopping bag.

With that kind of service, her business grows rapidly, as does her family of five sons and one daughter.

When her sons finish their education, they assume more responsibility and the little downtown Montreal store becomes the first link in an enormous Steinberg chain that includes many other businesses. The stores become so popular in Quebec that it is common to hear people say they are going Steinberging no matter where they plan to buy their groceries.

A vast empire of Steinberg grocery stores and Miracle Marts celebrate their golden anniversary during Canada's Centennial year in 1967 but sadly, with Ida and son Sam gone, family feuding sets in. The once dominant chain begins to decline and is sold for well over a billion dollars.

Some segments of the Steinberg chain still exist under different names today but clearly the glory days are over.

My father was commissioned by some members of the Steinberg family to author a book about Ida and her smile and apples, but for some reason he was asked to cancel the project just as he was about to finish.

He was never given a reason for the change of heart but always suspected it was because some members of the family didn't want the public to learn about Ida's humble beginnings. If that is true, what a shame, because the Ida Steinberg story is the quintessential Canadian success story of hard work, honesty, perseverance and overcoming challenges. Stories that should be told.

CANADA 150

THE GREAT TOOTH YANKER

In the classic movie "The Paleface", Bob Hope plays a wild-west dentist named Painless Potter, a slight adaptation of the name and character of one of the zaniest and most successful Canadians ever. A man, who by the way did not marry Calamity Jane (played by Jane Mansfield) as did Hope's rendition in the movie.

Edgar Randolph attends a Baptist seminary in New Brunswick before deciding there's more money pulling teeth than saving souls.

He receives his degree in dentistry just as we enter the 20th century, then sets out to make his fortune. Only for Edgar, fortune through normal channels is dragging its heels.

It's a time when the only painkiller is rotgut whiskey, which according to some, is as terrible as and even more dangerous than any toothache.

Business is slow for Edgar until, in desperation, he takes to the road calling himself Painless Parker. With the aid of a few molars up his sleeve and a couple of assistants who can moan and groan with toothaches something awful, Painless Parker is an immediate success.

When his moaners and groaners are supplemented by vaudeville acts, dancers and singers, he becomes the toast of North America, entertaining and yanking teeth from coast to coast.

He makes his fortune in only five years, retiring in 1905, but showbiz is in his blood.

It's not long until Painless is launching his career again with an even bigger circus of publicity, opening a chain of offices and practicing his mixture of magic, vaudeville and dentistry until he is 80.

A special law is passed at one point, requiring all dentists to use their real name. Undaunted, Edgar Randolph goes to court and legally changes his name to Painless.

If this story prompts you to have as look at "The Paleface" movie please be warned.

In it, Bob Hope sings one of the worst songs ever to win an Academy Award—Buttons and Bows! Awful!

YOU'RE NOT LEGAL,
YOU'RE A WOMAN!

Canada's first female lawyer is refused admission to law schools for many years because she is legally not a person. As a matter of fact, in those days neither was any other woman in the Country.

Even though Canada had been a country for 23 years, Clara Brett Martin is refused permission to study law anywhere in the Country because she and all other women in 1890, are by legal definition, not qualified as persons. In other words 23 years after Confederation, women are not legally persons.

Clara refuses to give up, petitioning the Law Society of Upper Canada again and again for admission to a university as a student at law.

Her case sparks heated debate, sometimes outright rage across the Country. The suffrage movements are just being launched and the realization that women are not legally persons under Canadian law is a particularly sore point.

Clara's case rages hot and cold for more than a year. Finally in 1892 an act is passed in Parliament permitting women to study law, but the Law Society of Ontario still refuses to allow it.

Clara then appeals to the Attorney General, Sir Oliver Mowat who finally rules in her favour.

It's not until 1897, fully 30 years after Confederation, that Clara Brett Martin is admitted to the Bar of Ontario, the first female lawyer, not just in Canada, but in the entire British Commonwealth.

At the turn of the century Clara is still Canada's only female lawyer, but before her death 23 years later, all provinces except Quebec allow women both to study and practice law.

All provinces today, thankfully have decided that women are legally people although it took Quebec longer than most to agree that women are actually real people!

THE WOMEN MEN!

"If women get the right to vote in Quebec they will become veritable women-men," says leading politician and newspaper owner Henri Bourassa.

"Women getting the vote cannot be justified by natural law or social interest," says Cardinal Louis-Nazaire Begin.

"Women voting would resemble a star having left its orbit," says leading politician Louis-Arthur Giroux.

With attitudes like those predominate in Quebec, small wonder it takes Therese Casgrain nearly 20 years of hard work to finally get women the right to vote in Quebec elections.

When Therese marries at the age of 18, Quebec women have fewer rights in many cases than animals. In fact the Quebec Civil Code classes women in the same category for legal purposes as minors, convicts, and idiots. Judging from the comments of people like Bourassa and the Cardinal it is a view widely shared by the ruling class of the day.

From 1928 until 1940 Therese Casgrain sponsors no fewer than 14 women's suffrage bills, all are defeated.

Finally on April 25, 1940, with thousands of women flocking to war plants and assuming vital roles, the Quebec National Assembly passes Bill 18 giving Quebec women the right to vote in provincial elections, long after the rest of Canada.

For the rest of her life Therese Casgrain works tirelessly fighting for women's rights. She battles both the Church and Premier

Maurice Duplessis in attempts to obtain equal pay for equal work, family planning education and equality in divorce courts.

Despairing of Liberal Party support she joins the CCF (the NDP today), and when elected leader of the Quebec Wing she becomes the first woman to head a political party in Canada.

She wins many honours and awards, including being named to the Senate by Pierre Trudeau even though they both know the appointment will be very brief since at the age of 74 she will have to step down as a Senator on her 75th birthday.

Therese Casgrain, one of those great Canadians whose face will surely soon appear on Canadian currency!

FORGET THE RED BARON!

Canada's most famous flying ace crashes his first aircraft when he is only 15! Mind you, the aircraft is one he makes himself of cardboard, wood crates and string. The flight is from the top of a three storey building. His sister has to dig him out of the wreckage but thank heavens, Billy Bishop is not seriously injured.

Yes, this is the same Billy Bishop who once shot down 25 enemy airplanes in just ten days then went on to form the RCAF. The same Billy Bishop after whom an airport on Toronto Island is named.

There is still some debate over who was the greatest air ace during the First World War, Canada's Billy Bishop or Germany's Red Baron. The supporters of the Red Baron claim he shot down 80 enemy aircraft during the war while Bishop's total was only 72. The question is how accurate is the German's claim of 80 kills? Some of them lack official verification, while all 72 of Bishop's victories were observed and recorded by at least one other witness.

Bishop's most spectacular feat is in 1917 when he singlehandedly attacks a German aerodrome, destroying two planes on the ground, then shooting four out of the air before running out of ammunition and having to flee with five German planes hot on his tail.

He is awarded the Victoria Cross for that accomplishment, then during the same year is promoted to captain, then to major. Not bad for a graduate of the Royal Military College in Kingston who started his career just a few years previous as a cavalry officer.

By the end of the War, Billy Bishop has been promoted to Lieutenant Colonel and in addition to the Victoria Cross has won the Distinguished Service Order and Cross, the Distinguished Flying Cross, the Legion of Honour and is made a Companion of the Order of the Bath on the King's Birthday Honours List of 1944.

Appointed to the staff of the British Air Ministry in 1918, Bishop forms the Royal Canadian Air Force as a separate brigade.

At the outbreak of the Second World War, Billy Bishop is again called upon to serve, this time as Honorary Air Marshall in charge of recruitment for the air force he formed some 20 years earlier.

Billy Bishop's decorations are now on display at the Canadian War Museum in Ottawa and the Air Marshall William Avery Bishop Museum is a major tourist attraction in his home town of Owen Sound, Ontario.

THE QUACKS!

The Yukon Gold Rush is on, a typhoid epidemic has broken out, it's a job for the newly formed Victorian Order of Nurses. The call goes out for volunteers. "You must be unmarried, at least 28 years old and be a graduate of a recognized nursing school," read the advertisements. Applicants are warned that they will have to dress very plainly and not curl or crimp their hair.

Four candidates are selected and are rushed north where they help save many lives.

It is exactly the kind of nursing care Lady Aberdeen had in mind when she formed the Victorian Order of Nurses (VON) on February 10, 1897 as a memorial for the 60th anniversary of Queen Victoria's ascent to the British Empire Throne.

Visiting nurses were desperately needed at that time in our history. Doctors were few and far between. Settlers in some of the more remote parts of Canada often had to wait days in terrible pain before being attended. Far too frequently women died in childbirth because there was no trained help.

But despite the need, the idea of a national association of visiting nurses met fierce opposition from many quarters. Sir Charles Tupper, who as Premier led Nova Scotia into Confederation and is a medical doctor himself once claimed, "These female quacks are dangerous. They're threatening the good health of the Nation!" He was not alone in those sentiments.

But fortunately Lady Aberdeen, born Isabel Marjorie Banks, now married to John Gordon, Lord Aberdeen, soon to become Canada's Governor General, is not easily dissuaded.

Under her leadership the VON grows into Canada's largest national homecare organization.

Today the VON employs 5,000 staff plus 9,000 volunteers and according to their website, "touches the lives of a million Canadians every year"!

By the way, Sir Charles Tupper got his just reward for his snarky remarks about female quacks. He holds the record for the shortest stay in office as Prime Minister. He was booted out after only 69 days. Even Kim Campbell with 101 days in office lasted longer than old Sir Charles!

THE EARLY BIRD

Did you know the only reason Casey Baldwin becomes the first Canadian and probably the first British subject to fly is because he forgot his skates?

"Wait a minute!" I can hear you say, "Wasn't John (J.A.D.) McCurdy the first Canadian to fly when he took the Silver Dart up over Baddeck, Nova Scotia?" Good question but the answer is simple.

The flight of the Silver Dart with McCurdy at the controls was on February 23, 1909, the first manned flight in the British Empire, but Casey Baldwin was actually the first Canadian to fly anywhere when he piloted the Red Wing over the ice of Lake Keuka near Hammondsport, New York a year before the Silver Dart.

Frederick W. (Casey) Baldwin was one of those absent-minded geniuses. He comes to visit Alexander Graham Bell for a few days and stays for 40 years.

Following several experiments with kites at Baddeck, Baldwin, Bell, McCurdy and Glen Curtiss, all members of the Aerial Experimental Association, move to Hammondsport to be near the Curtiss Engine Factory (yes, same Curtiss).

Bell is off to Washington March 8, 1908 when McCurdy, Curtiss and Baldwin wheel the "Red Wing" out onto the ice of Lake Keuka for what becomes an historic flight.

McCurdy and Curtiss have strapped skates onto their feet, but Baldwin has simply not gotten around to finding his. Baldwin can hardly stand up on the ice, so as the least useful member of the team he is strapped into the cockpit.

Curtiss starts up the motor, he and McCurdy grab the wings while Baldwin revs her up then shouts "Okay let's go!" The men jump back. The "Red Wing" taxis across the ice for 150 feet and leaves the ice. Baldwin pulls her nose up and she soars to a height of between four and five feet.

She flies for 319 feet before the motor conks out and she crashes back to earth.

Baldwin thus becomes the first Canadian to fly and since the flight of the "Red Wing" is open to the public, unlike the almost secret flights being carried out by the Wright Brothers, the Red Wing receives widespread press coverage and greatly encourages the team to return to Baddeck and build an even better airplane which they will call the Silver Dart!

MIGHTY MICE!

St. Patrick rids Ireland of snakes, the Pied Piper marches the rats out of Hamelin, and in Prince Edward Island an Indian shaman banishes the invading mice hordes!

It's the mid 18th century, the white population of Prince Edward Island comprises about 350 French farmers and fishermen who are just getting nicely settled and beginning to prosper.

The soil along the north shore, near what is now the thriving tourist area of North Rustico is extremely fertile, crops seem to almost leap from the ground.

Suddenly, without warning and for no apparent reason, from the surrounding woods spring millions of field mice. They advance like a mighty and devastating army in long narrow columns. They devour everything, even small trees that lie in their path.

The march continues for days, all the way from Malpeque to East Point, they wipe the face of the Island clean and leave nothing behind except rocks and stumps.

Crops are destroyed, the residents are reduced to eating fish and game. Next spring there is no seed to sow. Many settlers must leave or starve.

The invading mice don't stop until they reach the Souris River! Wait a minute! Souris, isn't that the French word for mouse? Yes it is. The English interpretation is the Mouse River and the lovely little town of Souris is, in English, the lovely little town of Mouse! Now you know how they got those names!

No sooner have the mouse invasions abated when a cloud of locusts descend and devour the crops once again.

A local Indian shaman comes forward with the solution, claiming that all the misfortune is because of an evil spirit hiding in a man he calls Perigord. The shaman insists Perigord must be killed and several days later reports back that the deed has been done with the body safely buried on a nearby island.

We have no idea who Perigord was, or whether, in fact, he was killed, but evil spirit or not, neither the mice or locusts ever return and the area has prospered ever since.

PIG PEN HISTORY

Just up the road from me is a falling down old log pig pen. What a story it could tell, if only it could talk. A story shared by many of the old log cabins now serving as pig pens or chicken coops throughout Eastern Ontario.

Because with rare exceptions, there was a time, not that long ago, when behind those logs was a pioneer family hacking a country out of forest, swamps and rocks.

It was the American Revolution which prompted most of the settlements in Eastern Ontario. Thousands of those in the 13 colonies that were soon to become the United States refused to join the Revolution and fight against the King. Abandoning everything they owned they fled north into Canada looking for land.

To accommodate the United Empire Loyalists (as they become known) the land along the St. Lawrence and Rideau Rivers is surveyed with townships of ten square miles established.

One seventh of this land is retained as Crown Land, another seventh is set aside as Clergy Reserves. The rest is granted to those who qualified. A Loyalist, his wife and each son and unmarried daughter at maturity are entitled to 200 acres.

Discharged soldiers receive land according to rank. Officers are entitled to no more than 1,000 acres on a river. The rank and file each get 200 acres.

The earliest settlers have to build their own rough log shanties. With luck in a few years they can organize a "bee" involving a dozen or more men who will build a new larger, but still log home for the family. Logs are cut according to the size of the cabin, usually 18 to 20 feet long.

If it is only a shanty it might have an eight foot high wall at the front, sloping to only four feet at the back with a dirt floor. Often the shanties are shared with farm animals during winter to help keep the place warm!

The roofs are usually made of basswood logs split in half and overlapping which is supposed to make it waterproof but usually doesn't. Some cabins have dirt floors, others have split basswood logs laid on the ground. Moss, bark, and clay are used to fill the chinks.

The cabin door is made of wood, the hinges of leather. The window glass is a gift from the Government—12 panes yearly for the first three years.

Furnishings are hauled over bush trails by oxen, but most items are made by the settlers' wives except for much prized feather filled pillows and straw filled mattresses. (Popular wedding gifts!) Bed springs are made from interwoven bark.

The next time you're driving around Eastern Ontario, especially in the Richmond, Carleton Place area, you will still see some of those early log cabins—usually now at the rear of a new modern home.

Pigs and chickens run in and out of those cabin doors these days, but there was a time when those tiny buildings were home to a sturdy, self-sufficient, incredibly tough people who forged a great Country out of bush and swamp.

Ah! If only those logs could talk!

CANADA 150

THE MAD PLOT

There's a desperate attempt to have pigs delay Newfoundland joining Canada but Joey Smallwood will have no part of it.

Few people are aware of it, but behind those crisp strips of frying bacon is a story of international politics and intrigue.

Let me explain.

Shortly after the Second World War, the Canadian Government sees that imported Danish bacon is rapidly gaining popularity because it tends to be leaner. Canadian pigs tend to be fatter than the famous Danish Landrace Hog, so the Canadian Government decides what we need is a longer, leaner Canadian breed of hog.

So the people who decide these things set out to create what they call a "National Pig" at the Experimental Farm in Lacombe, Alberta. In a burst of creativity they will call this new pig, when it is finally developed, "The Lacombe".

Among those who think this idea is crazy is the editor of Canada's national farm magazine, the Family Herald. His name is H. Gordon Green, who happens to be my late father.

Green argues that instead of spending millions trying to develop an entirely new breed of hog we should instead just import and breed the pig that is stealing all of our markets—the Danish Landrace Hog, which is so long and lean it has an extra set of ribs. (More space for bacon!)

The Government reaction to this is incredibly, passing a law making the importation of any Danish pigs illegal.

Green goes ballistic and sets out immediately to break the law and bring some of those famous Danish pigs into Canada and be damned with the consequences.

What follows are several years of intrigue. At one point he gets some Landrace into England where they are promptly stolen. A growing number of Canadian farmers join his cause, various bribes are offered, all to no avail.

Then Green gets a brainwave! Newfoundland has just voted to join Canada. The date is set for midnight March 31, 1949. If he can get some of the outlawed pigs into Newfoundland while it is still a British colony, then when it enters Confederation, the pigs will automatically be living in Canada!

There's just one problem. His source in Denmark says he can't get the pigs shipped until mid-April at the earliest.

So Green phones Joey Smallwood in Newfoundland and tries to persuade him to delay joining Canada for a month, until the end of April. "Joey was a pig farmer himself", explains Green, "he, of all people, should understand the importance of this."

Joey Smallwood will have none of it. "I will not delay Confederation for a few pigs," he says.

As the record shows, Newfoundland joins Canada as scheduled, midnight March 31, 1949. The great "pig plot" fails!

Green finally does smuggle some of those Danish pigs into the County however. Canadian authorities make all sorts of threats but in the end common sense prevails, the government relents and allows the legal importation of Danish Landrace Hogs. The great "Lacombe National Pig Project" is scrapped.

Within a few months many more Landrace Hogs pour into Canada until today almost every hog raised in Canada has at least some Landrace blood in them and it is now Canadian bacon that is world famous. (Didn't John Candy star in a movie about Canadian Bacon?!!!)

Years later I interview Joey Smallwood on my radio show and ask him about that phone call from H. Gordon Green.

He looks at me through those owl glasses of his. "That was your father!" I nod, "Yes it was."

"I thought the man was mad," says Joey.

CANADA 150

THE ALMOST PIG WAR

I know it's hard to believe, but things were so strained between the United States and Canada in the years just prior to Confederation that we almost went to war with each other over one skinny little pig!

The Oregon Treaty which defined the 49th parallel as the border between what is now British Columbia and Oregon was supposed to have settled the long brewing feud over the boundaries but the experts made one little mistake in drawing up the lines. They forgot about the small island of San Juan, just off the BC coast.

Since Confederation is still a few years off, it is the British who lay claim to the Island. So does the United States. Tempers flare.

Oregon tries to collect taxes from the Hudson's Bay Company which keeps cattle, pigs and a few sheep there. There are also a number of American settlers on the Island who continually quarrel with the British.

One day a small pig owned by the Hudson's Bay Company wanders into one of the American gardens, gobbles up some potatoes, and is shot for his efforts.

The Hudson's Bay Company, which is refusing to pay taxes to Oregon, rubs salt into the wounds by demanding $100 in damages for the shot pig.

The American settlers refuse to pay and send a petition to Major General William Harney, commander of U.S. forces in Oregon.

To understand the gravity of the situation you've got to understand what a monster General Harney was. And monster is exactly how many newspapers of the day described him after he whipped a female slave to death and committed several horrific atrocities against native Indians.

There is little doubt, that if he had his way, he'd wipe any British, not only off San Juan Island, but off the face of the planet.

Knowing Harney's reputation, the British send five warships to stand guard just off the Island.

If one shot had been fired in anger, all-out war would surely have broken out but cooler heads prevailed.

Stationed on the Island are 461 American soldiers with 14 cannons.

Offshore are five British warships with 70 cannons and 2,140 troops!

Both sides have been warned not to fire the first shot, but told if fired upon, open up with everything you've got.

Soldiers spend several days shouting insults back and forth at each other trying to get the opposing side to fire the first shot.

Finally U.S. President James Buchanan decides that going to war against Britain over one dead pig doesn't make much sense. A truce is declared with an agreement that a third party will settle ownership.

As it turns out, it's Kaiser Wilhelm I of Germany who, after considering the case, finally deeds San Juan Island to the United States in October, 1872.

History doesn't tell us whether anyone ever got paid for that poor pig!

Once again war is averted!

CANADA 150

THE ANGEL OF LONGPOINT

Abigail Becker! What an incredible woman! There is just no other way to describe her. You've probably never heard of her but in the minds of many who have studied her life, she is truly one of the greatest heroes this Country has ever seen. Why her picture isn't on Canadian currency or at the very least a stamp is beyond me.

Long Point, Ontario, jutting out into Lake Erie is a popular summer cottage community now but when seventeen year old Abigail Becker moves there about a decade before Confederation, it is a desolate, almost deserted, windswept, storm-lashed sand bar, the scene of many shipwrecks.

But from all reports Abigail loves it. She marries a widower, but looking after his six children doesn't stop her from exploring Long Point and the many sand bars which surround it.

So when the three-masted schooner "The Conductor" out of Buffalo runs aground in a vicious storm, Abigail knows she can reach the stricken sailors who have lashed themselves to the rigging as the ship slowly settles into the Lake.

Abigail's husband is away when the wind dies enough for her to hear the cries for help so she sets out on her own to rescue the men she knows must be half frozen to death in the late November cold.

Although she cannot swim, she ventures out into the bitterly cold water, wading up to her chin over several sand bars until she is within shouting distance of the stricken ship. She tries to convince the desperate men that the water is not deep, that they can wade to safety but the men are only semi-conscious from the cold and cannot move.

One by one Abigail unties the men from the mast, hoists them onto her shoulders and carries them to safety. Sometimes she is completely submerged in the icy water. All eight lives are saved.

Her fame quickly spreads when a few months later, four exhausted and half frozen sailors show up at her door, survivors of a ship that sank nearby. When they tell her that two of their companions are still outside having given up trying to save themselves, Abigail and two of her boys brave a wild snowstorm, find the missing two and carry them to safety—all six survive.

Several medals are presented. The City of Buffalo awards her $350. The Prince of Wales (later King Edward VII) meets her and presents a gift. Queen Victoria sends her a handwritten letter of congratulations and a 50 pound reward.

When her husband is drowned during a storm, Abigail who had eight children with him raises 14 children on her own then a few years later marries again and has three more children.

The Canadian band Tanglefoot writes a song about her—books have been written, but sadly today this truly great Canadian hero is mostly forgotten. Should we start a campaign to get her picture on some Canadian currency? Which bill should it be?

THE GREAT SPIRIT

One of the great mysteries surrounding the settlement of North America by Indians is how so many of the different tribes not only speak a similar language but share a version of the same Great Spirit they call Manitou or Gitche Manitou.

What isn't generally known is that the word Algonquin does not apply to just one tribe of aboriginals, but rather an entire group of Native North Americans comprised of many different tribes stretching from Canada's east coast to Manitoba and even into the midwestern United States. All members of this very large group speak a similar language and have some version of Manitou as their supreme being.

Several tribes who lived in what is now Ontario believe that the Great Spirit Manitou created Manitoulin Island by scooping out Georgian Bay and hurling it at some escaping evil spirits.

The province of Manitoba is named after Lake Manitoba which derives from the Cree or Ojibway name of manitou-wapow, referring to the sound of the waves crashing against rocks.

Whiteshell Provincial Park in Manitoba contains a number of ancient petro forms which the local Anishnaabe Midewiwin Tribe have named Manito Ahbee, the place where God sits.

On our east coast, Micmac folklore says that Glooscap, the incarnation of Manitou, came to see his people of the light, so named because they are the closest to the sunrise. He anchored his great stone canoe which turned into an island covered with trees, Prince Edward Island.

The legend is that Glooscap created man by shooting off pieces of bark from trees. He then created birds and animals which at first could speak Micmac. The loons were his messengers and one day when Glooscap was old and feeble the loons came flying to him with news of strange pale-faced men coming from across the sea in boats much larger than Indian canoes.

Glooscap knew then his reign was over and he must sail westward, alone.

Today, according to legend, Glooscap sits in his long tent in the happy hunting ground, making arrows for his last great battle. When his tent is full of arrows he will return to overcome the white man and bring back the golden age of happiness for the Micmac.

The loons, to this day, are still Gooscap's messengers. They make their strange and lonely calls because the news is still all bad!

THE CATALOGUE

Hard to believe but there was a time, not that long ago, when you could buy a brand new car for $300 without having to go near a dealership! In any colour as long as it was black! Not only that, but you could have it delivered to your home complete with driving instructions!

If you happen to have the 1926 edition of the T. Eaton catalogue you'll see it there. A brand spanking new Model T Ford in the latest colour, black, delivered to your home for $300.

The Model T was Henry Ford's great idea, make a car that the average working class man could afford, but the idea to advertise it in a catalogue was entirely that of the owner of a Toronto dry goods store. A man by the name of Timothy Eaton.

His was a simple enough idea but revolutionary at the time: Sell goods at fixed prices and offer a refund if they didn't suit the customer. It was an idea that made a multi-millionaire out of the man who conceived it and launched one of the largest commercial enterprises in the world.

In 1867, the year of Canada's Confederation, Timothy Eaton opens a small dry goods store at the edge of Toronto. Most people think it will be an instant failure because not only is the store far from the main commercial district of King Street, but his idea of selling for a fixed price then promising a refund if the goods aren't satisfactory just isn't the way business works in those days.

It is a time when haggling is the order of the day, and a refund? Unheard of.

But Timothy Eaton tries it and we all know what happened. Commercial practice is revolutionized and one of the most successful department store chains in the world is launched employing 70,000 people at one time.

It isn't long until Eaton tries something else that is revolutionary—huge catalogues sent to almost every home in Canada. Catalogues offering everything for sale from fur coats to socks, horse harnesses to hay forks, milking machines to yes, automobiles. It's been said, with considerable truth, that many families lived from birth to death without ever once entering a store of any kind. Their food was home grown, everything else was ordered through Eaton's catalogue.

In a time of outdoor privies, the catalogue itself served another useful purpose that some of you "old timers" know only too well!

THE VIRGIN MARY

By far the most spectacular event ever held in Ottawa was to honour the Virgin Mary and pray for world peace.

Until the Papal Mass of 2009 with 400,000 in attendance the 1947 Marian Congress at Lansdowne Park saw the largest attendance of any event ever held in the Capital, but for sheer spectacle nothing but nothing comes close to matching the Marian Congress.

At a time when Ottawa's population is only about 200,000, an estimated quarter of a million Roman Catholics flood into the Capital to take part in the five day event.

To accommodate the huge crowds, a special outdoor building is erected, 515 feet long and along its back wall are four large statues of angels raising gold trumpets towards a 115 foot high statue of the Virgin Mary.

Beneath the statue are a stage, altar, and benches for 75,000 worshipers.

During the Congress there is a procession of floats along the Canal Parkway including another huge statue of Mary. Tens of thousands watch. At its conclusion the traffic takes several hours to clear.

In attendance at the Congress are nine cardinals, 19 archbishops and 150 bishops from seven countries.

Prime Minister Mackenzie King hosts a special dinner for the cardinals. Dozens of leading politicians including Premier

Maurice Duplessis of Quebec, the Premier of Nova Scotia and Paul Martin, Minister of Health and Welfare attend some of the masses which at times are so crowded that one celebrant complains he has to sit through three masses before he can make his way out of the building.

One of the highlights of the Congress is the appearance of the 13 year old Dionne Quintuplets who sing hymns in both English and French. It's estimated more than 100,000 jam into the building to see them.

The Pope isn't there but broadcasts a radio message that is carried by all radio networks across the Country.

The whole event is concluded with a fireworks display which has been described as the largest, most spectacular ever seen.

Sadly, while the Second World War was over, none of the prayers brought us world peace!

STRONG, TOUGH WOMEN

Klondike Mike may have carried a piano over the Chilkoot Trail, but the Ottawa Valley's Jane Potter frequently hoisted a 100 pound bag of wheat onto her shoulders and lugged it six miles through bush and swamp, with several children in tow for a shopping trip to Richmond, ON.

Then, of course was the trip back from Richmond, this time laden down with tea, sugar and other supplies, always with the understanding that she would be back home in time to cook dinner.

From what we understand, Sam and Jane Potter were United Empire Loyalists who fled north into Canada to escape the ire of those Americans who had joined or supported the revolution against the British Crown.

Much of the Ottawa and Rideau Valleys were settled either by the "Loyalists", or by British soldiers no longer needed after fighting in the Napoleonic Wars.

Much has been written and songs composed about the hardships endured and the feats performed by the men who pioneered and settled Canada, but if the truth be known, in many cases the women had to be even tougher, stronger, more courageous and hard-working than the men.

To begin with, in most cases, the women were younger than the men they married and often had to endure childbirth with little if any assistance and not even aspirin to dull the pain. Ancient Canadian graveyards are filled with tombstones identifying women who died before their 25th birthday!

The women, like the men, had to endure the terrible mosquitoes and blackflies without the aid of "Off". They were often just as handy with a gun, an axe and hayfork as any man and of course were not only in charge of feeding their ever growing families but had to hand make virtually everything from soap to bedsprings.

It was usually the women, as well, who insisted that schools be built for their children and encouraged the construction of churches.

Fairly typical is my Grandmother Green who, with my two year old father in tow, six months pregnant, husband incapacitated with a broken leg, living in a miserable, drafty chicken house on the Saskatchewan Prairie kept them all alive during the vicious winter of 1914 by shooting, cleaning, and cooking jackrabbits!

THE "KING"

It was a horse whose owner once bet to finish last that starts the Toronto Maple Leafs on the road to becoming one of hockey's greatest dynasties. Until recently of course!

Rare Jewel is a two year old filly owned by Connie Smythe who has just bought a Toronto hockey team he renames the Maple Leafs. In five starts, Rare Jewel finished last except for one race where she finished second last. As luck would have it, Smythe bet on her to finish last in that race as well, so Rare Jewel isn't one of Smythe's favourite creatures.

During the winter however, the horse begins to improve a bit and a decision is made to enter her in one of the most famous races of the day—the Coronation Stakes.

Smythe doesn't think she has a ghost of a chance and is at the wicket about to place a healthy bet on the favourite Frothblower when a man he doesn't like very much, slaps him on the back and shouts loud enough for everyone to her, "Frothblower all the way, eh Connie?"

"Give me 20 across the board on Rare Jewel," retorts Connie and sure enough, against all odds, Rare Jewel wins.

Connie picks up $10,000 in winnings, enough to be used as a down payment to acquire from the Ottawa Senators, the best defencemen in the league at the time, King Clancy.

The same King Clancy who helped the Ottawa Senators win the Stanley Cup in 1923 and again in 1927.

He joins the Leafs in their brand new home Maple Leaf Gardens in 1930 and two years later is the star player when the Maple Leafs win their first Stanley Cup and the rest as they say is history.

Whatever happened to Rare Jewel we don't know.

Did she ever win again? When asked, Connie Smythe said he didn't think so but that once was enough!

THE WORLD DOESN'T END

Niagara Falls sends Canadians flocking to their churches in anticipation of the end of the world.

Panic starts when a gale strikes Lake Erie in the spring of 1848. Debris piles up at the mouth of the Niagara River, effectively damning its flow for about 24 hours. Barely a trickle of water dribbles over the famous Falls.

The word spreads quickly throughout the Niagara area that the world is coming to an end. Thousands flock to church. One minister later claims more souls are saved in one hour than in the previous five years.

But not everyone spends all this time in church prayer.

Millers along the River make repairs to the parts of the mill normally under water. The captain of the "Maid of the Mist" steamer takes his men out and dynamites several rocks that have been bumping the ship's keel. Sightseers walk through the gorge and find muskets American troops threw away while crossing the River following the Battle of Lundy's Lane.

The next day the water flow reverts to normal. The world doesn't come to an end. Church pews are emptied.

Actually it's not the first time the Niagara Gorge is dry. It was that way some 25,000 years ago. The Niagara River back then was where the Dundas Valley is now. In fact, the River's flow actually hacked out that valley, but during the ice age the Dundas Valley route was blocked off by the ice and debris until a new waterway was carved out—the Niagara River.

Incidentally, since the Ice Age, the Niagara River has eaten its way back from where you now see it by a distance of about seven miles. The erosion is still underway. Each year the Falls moves westward about two and a half feet!

THE GODSEND!

Yes, Winnipeg lays claim to the world's biggest mosquitoes but its biggest problem is the fact that the Red River which cuts through the heart of town flows north and is very young.

The Red springs to life a bit south of Fargo, North Dakota and forms the boundary between that state and Minnesota. Because it flows north, very often it means that while the ice and snow may be melting in the southern portion, it is still frozen further north. It empties into Lake Winnipeg, but if the Lake is still frozen solid the River can't empty and thus floods its banks farther south, something that occurs very frequently.

The other problem is that while flowing through some of the flattest landscape in the world it is so young (about 9,500 years old) that it has not had time to dredge out a very deep path making overflowing its low banks very easy.

During the "Great Flood of 1997", more than 20,000 people just to the south of Winnipeg were forced to evacuate their homes. The cities of Grand Forks, North Dakota and East Grand Forks, Minnesota were completely submerged by the River which peaked there at an incredible 49 feet, 20 feet above flood level. Damage in those cities alone exceeded $2 billion.

Heaven only knows what would have happened in Winnipeg, probably mass evacuations and billions of dollars in damages, were it not for what locals used to call Duff's Ditch, or Roblin's Folly.

Despite tremendous opposition, Premier Duff Roblin, immediately following the terrible flood of 1950, ordered a huge trench to be dug around Winnipeg to divert some of the water from the Red River away from the City.

The ditch, officially called the Floodway, taps into the Red south of Winnipeg, skirts around the City's eastern edge for more than 47 kilometres then empties back into the River well to the north.

Started in 1962 and completed four years later at a cost of $63 million, it has a minimum depth of 24 feet and can bleed off a tremendous volume of water. During the height of the 1997 flood "Duff's Ditch" was diverting 60,000 cubic feet of water a second. The River itself has a capacity of 75,000 cubic feet of water a second so you can understand the vital role played by the "Ditch" in averting a disastrous flood in downtown Winnipeg.

They don't call it Duff's Ditch anymore or Roblin's Folly. After the City escaped the brunt of the '97 flood if you asked anyone in Winnipeg what they thought now about Roblin's Folly, they almost unanimously responded, "it's no ditch, it's no folly, it's a godsend!"

THE REPUBLIC OF CANADA

Yes, there was once a Republic of Canada with its own flag and currency. It didn't last long though—only 39 days.

Picture it! It's now 61 years since that historic date, July 4, 1776, that the United States declares its independence from Britain but here in Canada we're still being ruled from England and a growing number of people think it's time for a change.

"The Americans fought for their independence and look how well that country is doing", argue people like William Lyon Mackenzie, a leading politician of the day and the first mayor of Toronto.

Tired of just talking about kicking the British out and establishing an independent country like the United States, Mackenzie launches a rebellion which quickly fails. Expecting a general uprising of the people, he apparently forgets that many Canadians have fled the United States because they opposed the revolution there and are loyal to the British crown.

Undaunted, Mackenzie leads a group of about 200 rebels to a small island in the Niagara River and declares that Navy Island is the new Republic of Canada. He promises 300 acres on the mainland to anyone who will join him plus $100. A few more young men join him. He establishes Republic of Canada currency and a flag featuring two stars on a black background.

The Americans are not unhappy to see this kind of dissent in a country they tried to capture a few years before so they don't object when an American steamboat called the Caroline is donated to the rebels so they can be supplied, mostly from the United States.

For some reason the British wait for almost a month before they decide to put a stop to this but finally on December 29, 1837 the Royal Navy captures the Caroline, sets her ablaze and sends her out to drift towards Niagara Falls. In the skirmish, one American is killed and in retaliation, the Americans capture a British steamer and set it on fire.

Once again war between the two countries threatens to break out, but early in January—only 39 days after declaring Navy Island to be the Republic of Canada, Mackenzie gives up and flees to Buffalo where he and his men are sentenced to 18 months in jail for breaching neutrality.

Some 30 years later, July 1, 1867 four provinces join to form the Dominion of Canada without a shot being fired or a single ship being set ablaze!

THE SONG MY PADDLE SINGS

West wind, blow from your prairie nest
Blow from the mountains, blow from the west,
The sail is idle, the sailor too;
O' wind of the west, we wait for you.
               Blow, blow!

I have wooed you so,
But never a favour you bestow,
You rock your cradle the hill between,
But scorn to notice my white lateen
I stow the sail unship the mast;
I wooed you long but my wooing's past;
My paddle will lull you into rest.
O' drowsy wind of the drowsy west,
               Sleep, sleep.

By the mountain steep,
Or down where the prairies grasses sweep!
Now fold in slumber your laggard wings,
For soft is the song my paddle sings.

The first four verses of the poem Pauline Johnson sold for $3.

One of the most famous of all poems written by a Canadian. A poem Pauline recites in highly dramatic fashion countless times on stages across North America and England.

What isn't generally known is that Pauline Johnson acquires her fame, not so much from the poems she composes, but rather her recitation of those poems during theatrical performances in front of large audiences in almost every village, town and city in Canada and the Eastern United States.

For 15 years, Pauline Johnson is one of the most popular performers in the English speaking world.

Beautiful and exotic looking she is loved by audiences, both native and white. When, during a private performance in London, she performs, with dramatic gestures and deep thrilling voice, her latest poem, "The Cattle Thief", Queen Victoria applauds long and loud.

Pauline's best known poem "The Song My Paddle Sings" sells for only $3 but by the time of her death in Vancouver in 1913 she can command almost any price for a guest appearance.

The daughter of an Indian chief and a British woman, she always considers herself an Indian, donating most of her income towards aboriginal causes.

Today you can see a monument to her in Vancouver's Stanley Park where her ashes are buried.

In 1961, the centennial of her birth, Pauline Johnson was honoured with a commemorative stamp bearing her image, thus making her the first woman, other than the Queen, to be so recognized.

Many schools across Canada bear her name and during the opening ceremonies of the 2010 Winter Olympics in Vancouver, Canadian actor Donald Sutherland read the following quote from her poem "Autumn's Orchestra".

> *Know by the thread of music woven through*
> *This fragile web of cadences I spin,*
> *That I have only caught these songs since you*
> *Voiced them upon your violin.*

THE ROBILLARD BOYS

Joseph Robillard fights off nine German airplanes to save his squadron leader's life!

Rocky Robillard survives more than 100 sorties flying bombers over Germany then becomes a famous athlete and sportscaster.

Joseph wins the Distinguished Flying Medal, the first French Canadian thus honoured!

Rocky sets scoring records in both hockey and football at McGill University and is named to its Sports Hall of Fame becoming one of the most famous personalities in Ottawa!

It's June 1942. There's heavy fighting over a major power station in northern France. Pilot Officer Joseph Robillard, at the controls of a Spitfire, sees his commanding officer bail out of his burning plane.

As the parachute billows out, several German planes begin firing at the dangling figure beneath. Robillard dives into the enemy formation shooting down two, but is attacked by nine. He manages to drive them off, but his machine is so badly damaged he's forced to crash land near Lille in Nazi occupied France.

Badly wounded, he is found by a group of local partisans and hidden until he recovers.

Then in a feat hard to imagine, Robillard, under the noses of the Germans, walks all the way across France to Gibraltar, is flown back to Britain and re-joins the fray.

He's credited with seven downed enemy aircraft and receives a hero's welcome back home in Ottawa.

After three years of flying Lancaster bombers over Germany, Rocky Robillard, (yes they are brothers) enrolls at McGill University where he captains both the hockey and football teams. On the gridiron he is an all-star running back, scoring 62 points in 18 career games but also plays quarterback and kicker. Just to make sure he's kept busy, he goes on to lead the McGill Redmen hockey team in scoring each of his final two years.

Upon graduation, Rocky coaches the Redmen for six years then becomes the assistant coach McGill's football team. After his coaching days Rocky returns to Ottawa where he becomes a well-known sportscaster with both CFRA Radio and CTV television. He is elected posthumously to McGill's Sports Hall of Fame in 2011, three years after his death.

THE TEACHER HERO

The first George Medal to commemorate brave action by civilians during wartime was won in Canada by an Alberta school teacher.

It's November 10, 1941, Mrs. Francis Walsh is teaching at the one room Big Hill Springs School near Calgary when suddenly out of the sky comes a tremendous roaring sound followed by a violent crash in the schoolyard.

Mrs. Walsh rushes outside to see a Gipsy Moth training airplane burning fiercely. A young man, his clothes afire and blood streaming from his face is staggering about the wreckage trying to free the pilot. Mrs. Walsh understands the problem immediately. It's clear the pilot is dead and the man trying to rescue him is in shock.

Shouting to one of the older boys to go for help, she braves the possibility of explosion, runs to the flaming man, and despite serious burns to her hands, arms and face, Mrs. Walsh rolls the airman on the ground and beats at the flames with her bare hands.

With the aid of her pupils, she carries him into the schoolhouse and administers first aid. A doctor arrives a few minutes later but not until he finishes treating the airman does Mrs. Walsh ask for assistance for her own injuries which are considerable and very painful.

Unfortunately the airman, Leading Aircraftman Karl Gravell dies in hospital but when Mrs. Walsh receives the George Medal at Rideau Hall two years later the citation reads, "She displayed great personal courage and coolness under circumstances which were entirely strange to her."

Mrs. Walsh is the first Canadian to win the Medal, struck by King George VI in 1940 to honour acts of great bravery not in combat throughout the British Commonwealth. Her only comment to the Governor General who presented the Medal was, "I only did what anyone would do under those circumstances!"

SHAMEFUL!

The manner in which Canada treated one of our greatest heroes is nothing short of disgraceful. You be the judge!

Thirty-nine year old Private Michael O'Rourke is a stretcher bearer throughout the fighting for "Hill 70" in August of 1917.

The battle for the Hill, not far from Vimy Ridge is one of the fiercest of the entire war. Nearly 3,000 young Canadian men are killed there in just three days.

Day by day, night by night, the tide of battle ebbs back and forth. The wounded lie thick upon the field but the stretcher bearers of the 7th Battalion are equal to the task.

For three days and nights, a sleepless Private O'Rourke, locates the wounded and carries them to safety. He is almost always under heavy fire. So dangerous is the stretcher bearers' work that in those three days, 16 stretcher bearers of the Battalion are reduced to just three able to carry on.

Once, O'Rourke is knocked down and partially buried by a shell, he digs himself out and continues his life saving work. Another time he sees a wounded comrade about 50 yards in front of the Canadian line, lying helpless in "no man's land". O'Rourke dashes through machinegun fire and rescues him.

On another occasion O'Rourke faces a storm of gunfire as he saves a wounded man who has been left behind in a listening post that was abandoned.

O'Rourke's bravest deed was rescuing a man stumbling about in the middle of "no man's land" blinded. The Germans, anticipating a rescue attempt, don't shoot at him. O'Rourke leaps over the parapet, zigzags through heavy fire, throws the man over his shoulder and miraculously makes it to safety.

Several of the men whose lives he saved, travel thousands of miles to be there when the King presents Private Michael O'Rourke with the Victoria Cross.

But that is pretty well the end of his reward because when he returns home he finds an ungrateful nation tired of war and its heroes.

He is forced to live on a disability pension of $10 a month and whatever he can earn as a part time worker on the docks of Vancouver. His last few years are spent forgotten, ignored and at times homeless.

It's the dirty 30's. No one can find work, the pay for back breaking work on the docks is a pittance. O'Rourke, wearing all his medals, leads a group of workers demanding better pay. They are met by 350 police armed with billyclubs, guns and tear gas. O'Rourke is beaten and gassed along with most of the rest of the men, even the VON volunteers who set up an aid station are gassed.

Although we don't know for sure, the belief is that O'Rourke had to sell his Victoria Cross for a few dollars needed for food!

A shameful chapter in Canada's history indeed!

GOOD LUCK—BAD LUCK

It`s the afternoon rush hour and Hwy 20 is backed up, worse than usual, all the way from Montreal to Dorval about 15 miles to the west. Motorists trying to catch TCA flight 831 to Toronto from Dorval Airport (Pierre Trudeau Airport today) are frustrated. The flight leaves at 6:28 p.m. and time is running out. Eight of them don`t make it to their gate in time. They miss their flight. It saves their lives!

One of those who does make it in time is Phil Lewis, a technical supervisor with the Polymer Corporation. Phil has a train ticket in his pocket for his home town of Sarnia, but it's his 39th birthday and at the last minute he decides to get home early for a celebration with his family. There are seats available on TCA flight 831 to Toronto so he books one and despite the terrible Friday evening traffic jam, makes the flight in time. It`s a decision that costs him his life.

It`s Friday November 29, 1963. Much of the world is still reeling in shock and horror from the assassination of President John F. Kennedy only one week before.

TCA flight 831 takes off from Dorval Airport exactly on time, 6:28 p.m. Four minutes later the DC8 slams into the foothills of the Laurentian Mountains. There are no survivors. All 111 passengers and seven crew members are believed to have died instantly. The wreckage is spread over several acres.

TCA flight 831 is the deadliest plane crash involving Canadians in our history and in terms of lives lost it is the third worst crash ever on Canadian territory.

On December 12, 1985, 256 American soldiers and aircrew died when Arrow Flight 1285 crashed near Gander, Newfoundland. And of course the crash of Swissair flight 111 MD-11 near Peggy's Cove, Nova Scotia which claimed 229 lives on Sept. 2, 1998.

A Department of Transportation inquiry ruled that the TCA crash was likely caused by mechanical failure of the pitch-trim compensator. This device regulates the nose up or down tendency of the aircraft.

There is a problem with that finding however, since several eyewitnesses claim they saw what one described as a "flaming ball" or "red streak" in the sky indicating either a fire or explosion just prior to the crash.

The Sarnia Historic Society webpage says, "People in Ste. Therese de Blainville recall seeing a flaming red streak in the sky plummeting to earth."

Noteworthy as well is that the findings of the inquiry used the word "probably" when affixing the cause! In those days, of course, no one even dreamed of the kind of terrorism we face today. What really happened aboard flight 831 we will probably never know.

THE CANOE UP THE CREEK PLOY!

I know it's hard to believe, but the Ontario Government, the Toronto sports media and a hard-core group of anti-sports local residents were so desperate to stop construction of a new arena for the reborn Ottawa Senators Hockey Club they actually did send a canoe up a creek to try and stop it!

Awarded an NHL franchise on Dec. 6, 1990, the Senators first took to the ice in 1992 and for the first four years played in a somewhat refurbished Junior A arena in downtown Ottawa called the Civic Centre. It was not an NHL arena.

The plan from the start was to immediately build a new state-of-the-art arena and hotel complex on 100 acres of vacant farmland about 20 miles west of the Capital.

The Ontario NDP Government with Bob Rae as Premier wanted no part of a new arena and was determined to stop construction and thus force the demise of the Senators. Joining the Government in trying to scuttle the upstart Senators was a good chunk of the Toronto media and in particular the sports media and sadly, a fair number of leading citizens in Ottawa and suburban Kanata where the arena was scheduled to be built.

For two years the battle waged between the Government and Bruce Firestone, President of Terrance Corporation which owned both the Senators franchise and the land for the arena.

Finally the mess ended up with the Ontario Municipal Board which ruled in favour of development, but imposed severe restrictions. Firestone was denied the right to build a hotel and seating was reduced in the new arena by almost 2,000.

The most severe blow and the thing which almost killed the entire project was that Firestone and the Senators were ordered to pay the full cost of building an overpass over Highway 417 and other connecting roadways. A roadway that provided access to hundreds of homes and dozens of businesses. A roadway that today serves a burgeoning new housing development and outlet mall!

When the federal government of the day which had provided free land for the construction of the Skydome (now Rogers Centre) offered to help in some way, the Toronto media raised such a fuss that the Feds had an almost overnight change of heart.

Despite all of this, it looked as though the Senators might survive and horror of horrors actually build a brand new arena.

Obviously this kind of progress had to be stopped so someone did some research and found that if the Carp Creek, which flows close to where the arena was to be built, was navigable, the land surrounding it would come under the jurisdiction of several different provincial and perhaps even federal departments, which of course would mean more long delays.

Since the Carp Creek most of the time can easily be spanned by a four year old leaping from bank to bank and is sometimes dammed by a dozy cow taking a nap in its cool waters, it was agreed a power boat would quickly run aground so, brainwave time. Someone came up with a brilliant idea. If even a canoe could be paddled up that creek it meant it could be navigated and that would put an end to the Senators and their crazy ideas once and for all.

So, believe it or not, with photographers, reporters, anxious Senators supporters and some representatives from the Bob Rae Government in attendance, a canoe was bravely launched with an expert canoeist at the paddle.

He didn't make it 100 yards. The canoe couldn't navigate up or down the creek, even with a paddle! The Senators lived for another day.

The new arena, called the Palladium, was officially opened on January 15, 1996. Featured in the stands was some wise guy with a large sign which read, "Carp Creek Yacht Club".

What really burned some of us who had fought hard for the new arena was that some of those who tried to kill the project were first in line for free tickets for the official opening ceremonies!

The Senators lost their first game played in the Palladium to the Montreal Canadiens, but in truth it was a huge victory against overwhelming odds.

THE DUELIST

Most school children learn that the Duke of Richmond died a horrible death from rabies near what is now the town of Richmond on the outskirts of Ottawa. At least it was taught during my school days. But what hardly anyone knows is that this is the same duke who as a young man, had not one, but two duels, including one where he seriously wounded his opponent.

His first duel was at the age of 23 in May of 1789 while he was a colonel in the Duke of York's regiment. We're not sure what the issue was, but rather incredibly Charles Lennox, who later became the 4th Duke of Richmond, issued a challenge to his commanding officer Frederick, the Duke of York.

The two of them face off against each other, pistols at the ready, on Wimbledon Common, yes the place where they hold tennis championships these days.

At the signal Lennox fires, the bullet grazing Frederick's head, but doing him no great injury. Frederick for some reason does not fire, perhaps believing that shooting at a man from a lower rank is beneath him.

A bit later that year a man named Theophilus Swift publishes a pamphlet critical of Lennox's character.

This time the combatants meet at dawn in a field near the Uxbridge Road. Both fire. Swift misses but is gravely injured when struck in the abdomen by the bullet from Lennox's gun.

History is a little vague about this, but while Swift did recover from his injury, only a couple months later Lennox marries the beautiful Lady Charlotte Gordon leading to speculation that the duel was over a woman, as many such duels were in those days.

Lennox must have had a short fuse, because not long after taking part in naval battles against the French in the West Indies he is sent home after what is described as coming into conflict with his superior officers.

It wasn't until after we entered the 19th century that Charles Lennox becomes the 4th Duke of Richmond when his uncle the 3rd Duke of Richmond dies.

Many adventures later Charles Lennox, the 4th Duke of Richmond is appointed Governor General of British North America, in other words Canada. Quite possibly because British authorities want to get him as far away as possible.

In the summer of 1819 the duke decides to have a good look at this country he rules and sets out to see as much of it as he can.

It is at Sorel, Quebec where he is bitten by a fox. Some reports talk about a pet fox, others believe it was wild. The wound appears to heal, so the duke proceeds on to Kingston then up the Rideau River to a little settlement that now bears his name. Here he becomes violently ill. He's taken to a barn where he dies a painful death from rabies.

Today dozens of streets, towns, schools and parks bear his name.

One of the barns at the annual Richmond Fall Fair, one of the largest such fairs in Eastern Ontario, is located almost at the exact spot where it is believed he died.

The Duke of Richmond's descendants and those of his 14 children include several members of British royalty.

MY FAVOURITE
DIEFENBAKER STORIES

John Diefenbaker with –left to right-CFRA News Anchor Don Leger,
Ottawa Carleton Regional Government Chair Andy Haydon, Ottawa
Mayor Lorry Greenberg and Lowell

My favourite story about former Prime Minister John
Diefenbaker involves the late Hal Anthony, one of Canada's
leading broadcasters and a dear friend.

Diefenbaker is signing his new book "One Canada" at a local
Ottawa bookstore and Hal, who is a great fan, buys the book and
joins the long lineup to have the "Chief" autograph his copy.

"Now to whom would you like me to address this?" asks
Diefenbaker. "Well if you don't mind Sir, could you make it out
to me, Hal Anthony?" It prompts an immediate reaction.

Dief looks up, his wattles dancing with excitement. "You're Hal Anthony!" Hal smiles, "Yes Sir, I'm a great fan!"

Dief gets up from his chair. "Let me shake your hand. My goodness Olive and I listen to you every chance we get, you are a wonderful broadcaster, wonderful, now don't you come from Saskatchewan?' "Yes Sir, Birch Hills, my father voted for you!"

This gets Dief really excited. "Oh yes, your father Mr. Anthony, I remember him well, is he still with us?'

"No Sir, he died some time ago." "Oh, I'm sorry to hear that, Mr. Anthony from Birch Hills, what a wonderful man, I remember him well. And your mother, Mrs. Anthony?"

Hal shakes his head. "We lost her only a couple of years ago." Diefenbaker sits down. "Oh I am sorry to hear that, Mrs. Anthony was a wonderful woman. The Anthony family I remember them all well, the Anthony family, I remember them very well— the Anthony family, a wonderful family, wonderful!"

At this, Hal's book is signed and he moves on not having the heart to, as he explains later, "tell the old bugger my family name is Bitz!"

He shows me his driver's licence and there it is as plain as day. Hal Anthony Bitz.

"The Bitz just didn't sound too good on radio," explains Hal. "There was no Anthony family, certainly not in Birch Hills!" And he laughs.

CANADA 150

MY SECOND FAVOURITE DIEFENBAKER STORY

It's Christmas Eve 1975. My guest on Ottawa Radio Station CFRA is John Diefenbaker, former prime minister and still MP for Prince Albert Riding in Saskatchewan. We talk a little politics but Dief doesn't appear to have much Christmas charity to extend to anyone on Parliament Hill, so we move on to something a little sunnier.

With only minor nudging, my guest launches into a bit of reminiscing about growing up on the Prairies and grows funnier and funnier. He rolls out story after story, some of them probably true, all the while chuckling away to himself.

Somehow we get discussing baseball and it turns out the man who was our 13th prime minister is a great fan of the New York Yankees and in particular Mickey Mantle.

Then he launches into the story that has stuck with me all these years.

"When I was a kid growing up in Prince Albert," he says, "we had a pretty good baseball team in town and I was crazy about some of the players. We didn't have any money in those days so I used to watch the games by peering through a large knothole in the wooden fence that surrounded the park."

Here he pauses for a moment and starts to chuckle again.

"One day I've got my eye glued to the knothole when the Chief Constable sneaks up behind me and gives me such a boot that it almost drives me through the fence onto the playing field!"

Here he gives a full throated laugh. "You know, I've often thought that if indeed I was launched through that knothole and someone asked me how I got in I would have told him I was assed in!"

MY THIRD FAVOURITE DIEFENBAKER STORY

It's a warm spring evening in 1965 when a petty criminal named
Lucien Rivard is given a garden hose and told to water the rink
at the Montreal prison. Somehow Rivard uses the hose to scale
the wall and escape. With charges of bribery floating about,
the escape creates a political nightmare for Attorney General
Guy Favreau who resigns in disgrace. A Royal Commission
is launched.

The consequences are nation-changing since, in order to erase
the stink of scandal and increase his popularity in Quebec, Prime
Minister Lester Pearson recruits three high profile Quebeckers
to join him—Jean Marchand, Gerard Pelletier and a man named
Pierre Trudeau! Otherwise known as the "Three Wise Men
of Quebec".

The situation is so sensational, the Canadian Press names Lucien
Rivard "Canadian Newsmaker of the Year". Songs are written.
One entitled "The Gallic Pimpernel" gets major radio play. Rich
Little brings the house down mimicking Pearson's voice singing
Old Man Rivard.

Later that year the Country is plunged into a federal election.
Prime Minister Pearson's Liberals up against the old warrior John
Diefenbaker, PC Party leader. What a show Diefenbaker puts on
at every rally. From coast to coast it's the same act.

Dief strolls up to the podium, peers up into the sky. The crowd
knows what's coming and starts to hoot and holler. Dief loosens
his collar, wipes his brow as if to flick the sweat away. The
crowd gets louder.

Dief starts shaking his head, looks to the sky again. "It was a night like this," he begins. The crowd almost in unision shouts. "Tell us, tell us."

He starts again. "It was a night like this," pause, "when they sent Lucien Rivard out to water the rink!'

The crowd goes nuts. Every time. Every place.

Priceless.

MY FOURTH FAVOURITE DIEFENBAKER STORY

You've heard of the Diefenbunker I am sure. Carp's main claim to fame. In fact Carp's only claim to fame. For strangers to the National Capital area, Carp is a lovely little village about 30 kilometres west of Ottawa, home to a 100,000 square foot underground bunker built to withstand a five megaton nuclear blast from 1.8 kilometres away.

It's a fascinating museum and library today, but when commissioned by Prime Minister John Diefenbaker in 1959 it was designed to accommodate 535 senior government and military personnel who hopefully would survive and be able to keep order in the event of a nuclear attack.

From 1961 until decommissioned in 1994, it was fully staffed by more than 100 people on a 24 hour shift rotation. The cupboards were constantly stocked with sufficient food and other supplies to last 535 people for 30 days. It was the site of some of Canada's most top secret communications throughout the Cold War.

Smaller bunkers but with a similar purpose were built in Nanaimo, BC, Penhold, AB, Shilo, MB, Borden, ON, Valcartier, QC, and Debert, NS. Much smaller ones were built in about 40 other locations.

There was just one problem with the Carp Diefenbunker. John Diefenbaker, then the Prime Minister of Canada, declared that, nuclear attack or not, he wouldn't move in unless his wife came with him.

The story is that upon completion, Dief was taken on a tour. He was very impressed until he reached a tiny room featuring a single bed which was reserved for him as Prime Minister. "Where will Olive sleep?" he asked.

"We're very sorry sir, but wives will not be accompanying husbands. Only 535 people deemed absolutely vital to the national interest will be allowed into the bunker in the event of an attack."

According to those present, the Prime Minister was taken aback. Shocked. "Olive won't be here with me? Is that what you are saying?" He asked.

The answer was in the affirmative.

"If that is the case," says Diefenbaker, "I will not be moving in here!" And he walks away. For years historians and journalists questioned whether that episode actually happened.

I know for a fact that some version of it did, because many years later during a Christmas Eve interview with an aging Diefenbaker I put the question to him.

"Did you or did you not tell the military that in the event of nuclear war you would not be joining them in the Diefenbunker if your wife was excluded?" I ask.

He pauses for a moment. "Yes I did say that!" "Did you mean it?" He nods, "At the time yes." He pauses again. I wait. "Fortunately," he says, "we didn't have to test my resolve did we?"

A HELLS ANGELS DIEFENBUNKER?

The giant Diefenbunker at Carp was designed to accommodate 535 leading government and military personnel for 30 days in the event of nuclear attack. Its construction was one of the best kept secrets of the Cold War. An even better kept secret, even today, is the fact that while the Carp installation was by far the largest, it is only one of about 50 much smaller bunkers built across the Country.

Most of these bunkers were built near major cities, each to accommodate at least a dozen people who would be in charge of whatever was left of those cities after a nuclear strike. Each had massive blast doors as well as extensive air filters and positive air pressure to prevent radiation infiltration. Underground storage was built for food, fuel, fresh water and other supplies.

Some of these smaller bunkers are sitting idle today. Some have been or are being refitted as museums. The bunker at Debert, NS used to serve as home base for a cadet gliding school but has recently been sold for use as a military museum.

The Diefenbunker at CFB Penhold in Alberta was decommissioned and sold to private interests.

When news got around that the Hells Angels biker gang was interested, believing it could easily be turned into an attack-proof headquarters, there was near panic in the streets!

The idea, as you can imagine, gave local residents nightmares and the Federal Government quickly moved in, bought the bunker and at great expense had it demolished and hauled away.

That's one of the problems with these Cold War relics. Because they were built to withstand a nuclear blast, tearing them down is a mighty tough task.

We were never told what it cost to hack the Penhold Bunker apart but you can be certain by the time everything was carted away the bill for it all was in the millions!

THE FLAME LIVES ON!

Four thousand Canadians save the famous Centennial Flame on Parliament Hill!

It's almost a year since our 100th birthday was ushered in by Prime Minister Lester Pearson lighting the newly completed Centennial Flame on Parliament Hill. But now we are being told the Flame will be extinguished as the clock strikes midnight signalling the end of our Centennial Year.

When I object on my radio show in Ottawa, Judy LaMarsh, the Secretary of State calls me personally to say that it was always the plan to extinguish the Flame to mark the end of our great birthday party. "The Flame will be extinguished during a special ceremony at midnight December 31,"she informs me.

I go on the air the next day with the information and the callers almost blow up the phone lines. "Look," says one young man, "this has been the greatest year in Canada's history, the Government has done almost everything right for a change; please don't tell me that the very last act of our Centennial Year is going to be one of stupidity!"

I launch a letter writing campaign. Thousands of letters pour into the offices of the Prime Minister, Works Minister George McIlraith and Ms. LaMarsh. More than 4,000 people sign a petition demanding that the Flame be kept burning. And don't forget, this is before the age of computers and the Internet! Mayor Don Reid and members of Ottawa City Council join the fray.

When some of the naysayers object to the cost, I work out a deal with Ottawa Gas to reduce the yearly cost of gas from the estimated $3,000 to just $1,700. I point out that more money than that was tossed into the Flame during the year so not only would that cover all costs but anything left over could be donated to charity.

In the midst of the campaign Judy LaMarsh calls me and says while she personally would like to preserve the Flame the final decision rests with Works Minister McIlraith.

I notify listeners of this plan the next day and urge them to keep the letters and phone calls pouring in.

Three days later Works Minister George McIlraith calls a special press conference to announce, "The Centennial Flame on Parliament Hill will be kept burning as a symbol of Canada's wonderful accomplishments during our first 100 years!"

Victory to the people!

THE WEDDING NIGHT VOW

A strange wedding night vow by an unhappy bride leads to the creation of Canada's first hospital!

As a child, Marie Guyart would far sooner play nun than house. She weeps openly and bitterly when a marriage is arranged for her with rich, but much older Claude Martin in 1616.

It's in her wedding bed that Marie, at the age of 17, vows that if she has a son she will dedicate him to the service of God. And should her husband die she will consecrate herself.

She is widowed only two years later after having a son, and spurning several marriage offers, the beautiful Marie enters the Ursuline Convent in Tours, France.

In her lonely cell there, Marie begins to hear voices and see visions instructing her to travel to far off Canada. She meets wealthy Madame de la Peltrie and persuades her to provide the necessary funds for a convent in the New World; and in 1639 both leave France for lives of incredible hardship and dedication in Canada.

In August of 1639 they establish Canada's first hospital at Sillery, Quebec and are almost immediately confronted with a horrible outbreak of smallpox among local Indians.

At one point after working without food or rest for three days and nights, Marie, now known as Marie de l'Incarnation, establishes the motto of what she calls her house of health, "We prefer death rather than desert our post."

The house of health was later moved to Quebec City and renamed Hotel Dieu.

In 1641, Marie and Madame De La Peltrie complete the first Mother House of the Ursuline Order in Canada and it was largely at Marie's urging that the first crops are planted and harvested.

It is the men who get most of the credit for founding our Country, but in fact it was the women like Marie Guyart who did much of the really hard work!

TWELVE FEET!

Henry Fuller Davis finds 12 feet and makes a fortune!

There's many a tale to be told of the men who moil for gold, but hardly a one that's any more fun that the 12 feet that shouldn't have been sold! (With apologies to Robert W. Service!)

Gold is the word on everyone's lips. The year is 1858, nine years before Confederation. Placer gold has been discovered in the Fraser Valley of British Columbia. More than 25,000 men pour into the Valley, staking every square inch of space. Even land beneath trees, houses and huge boulders is staked. One man makes a fortune digging beneath his bedroll in his tent.

By the time Henry Fuller Davis arrives, even the local graveyard has been staked out, but Henry immediately goes to work, not with a pick and shovel but with a tape measure.

It doesn't take him long to find what he's looking for, two claims, side by side, which are in excess of regulation width; between them is a free space of just 12 feet. But what a 12 feet!

From this he extracts a fortune in gold and becomes a legend throughout the land.

But "12 Foot Davis", as he becomes known, is more than just lucky.

In addition, he is a pioneer explorer helping to discover other important gold finds in northern Alberta and as a fur trader he helps establish settlements at Dunvegan, Hudson Hope, Lesser Slave Lake and Fort Vermillion.

His friendliness to pioneers, travellers and Indians becomes almost as legendary as his 12 foot fortune and on his tombstone overlooking the Peace River is the inscription:

"He was everyman's friend and never locked his cabin door".

THE SOOTHSAYER

It's 1904, black rust threatens the western wheat crop. Suppliers refuse to ship vital equipment to farmers. Credit is refused. Bankruptcy faces many.

It's a job for "Supersoothsayer" otherwise known as author, journalist and women's rights advocate, E. Cora Hind, whose ability to forecast wheat crops is a worldwide phenomenon.

For years, Cora's wheat crop predictions are so accurate they influence the stock market.

The atmosphere is tense as everyone awaits her prediction in 1904. There have been some reports of dreaded black rust which can spread like wildfire and destroy hundreds or even thousands of acres of wheat.

Then comes the news. The wheat crop will be good! No black rust!

The West goes wild with delight. Suppliers ship equipment, the banks loosen the reins on loans, the stock market surges.

As luck will have it, Cora is right again. It's not a bumper crop in 1904 but a good one.

Cora claims her predictions are magic, but in fact they are accomplished by hard work. Living in Winnipeg and as Agriculture Editor of the Winnipeg Free Press, Cora has access to a great deal of information and in addition, travels widely throughout the west, walking into wheat fields, checking up close and personal, examining the stalks, smelling and tasting them before making her predictions.

News of her ability spreads and she is invited to take part in a 27 nation examination of wheat crops around the world.

But it is not just with the agricultural community that Cora plays a major role. Her fame and prestige, in no small way, greatly assist in advancing the cause of women's equality.

She joins Nellie McClung in forming the Political Equality League of Manitoba, demanding voting rights for women at a time when women aren't even considered legal persons.

Soothsayer or not, E. Cora Hind is a key player in persuading Manitoba to become the first province in Canada to allow women to vote. (January, 1916).

When Cora Hind dies on October 6, 1942, trading at the Winnipeg Grain Exchange is halted for two minutes in her memory. The United Grain Growers create the Cora Hind Fellowship for research in agriculture and the Winnipeg Free Press creates the Cora Hind Scholarship in home economics.

You'll find her picture and story in the Manitoba Hall of Fame today, the only soothsayer thus honoured!

THE LAST CHANCE

Two young men pause beside a small stream not far from the Fraser River in British Columbia. They have been prospecting for gold during the great Cariboo Rush but have found nothing but disappointment and despair. They are broke, hungry and defeated. Their last digging is a day's walk behind them as they head home.

In a moment they will find riches beyond their wildest dreams.

The two men sit on an old log gazing at the beautiful hills around them. It's getting too late to go much farther that day so one of them suggests they give prospecting one last chance before making camp. "I'm game," says the other man, "but where?" His companion points to an outcropping just upstream. "Well that looks as good a spot as any."

Leaving their packs by the trail, they pick their way up the small creek and begin to dig in the gravel. They dump a shovelful of it into their pan, swirl it about in the water and begin to scream.

The bottom of the pan is covered with gold!

Frantically they stake out their claim and while one rushes to file it in Barkerville, the other continues to dig. In a few weeks, they go home with more than a quarter of a million dollars each.

We don't know the men's names, but their little creek is still there bearing the name they gave it—"Last Chance Creek".

CANADA 150

THE STRAIGHT SHOOTER

Canada's most decorated war hero learned to shoot straight from the back of a horse!

Young William Barker, "Will", loved to ride horses over the vast open plains of his childhood near Dauphin, Manitoba and he loved to shoot. He became such a crack shot while riding at full speed that one biographer suggests he could easily have become a trick shooter in a circus. While a good student he is frequently forced to take days off to go hunting. Even as a teenager his job is to hunt wildlife to provide food for the workers at his father's sawmill.

It is a skill that serves him well as he battles enemy aircraft over the fields of France and Italy during WWI.

One of his most successful battles, fictionalized by Ernest Hemingway in the short story, "The Snows of Kilimanjaro" is on December 25, 1917. Catching the Germans off guard he and Lt. Harold Hudson, his wingman, shoot up an airfield, setting fire to one hangar and damaging four enemy aircraft before dropping a placard wishing their opponents a "Happy Christmas".

But the battle that wins him the Victoria Cross is on October 27, 1918. The following is an official account of that day:

Barker spots an enemy two seater over France. He attacks and sends it plummeting to earth. But a Fokker sneaks up from the rear and opens fire. Barker is wounded in the thigh, but wheels around in time to rake his attacker which bursts into flame.

Barker then finds himself surrounded by enemy aircraft. Although badly wounded he once again manages to drive two of them into fatal spins. At this point, Barker, suffering from exhaustion and loss of blood, loses consciousness and his machine falls out of control. But before he crashes, he recovers and finds himself once again being attacked from all sides.

Barker singles out one plane, deliberately charges it head on, guns blazing. It is driven down in flames. Barker is wounded again, this time his left elbow is shattered and again he loses consciousness for a moment, recovering once again. He dives at yet another enemy plane, destroying it. The Germans recognize him as an "ace" and intensify their attacks.

Barker continues to fight, damaging several other planes, then finally is able to escape and land behind allied lines. Men of the RAF Balloon Section rush him to a field hospital. Transferred to a hospital in Rouen, France he fights for his life for nearly a year, finally being transported back to England in mid-January 1919.

He is not fit enough to walk the necessary few paces to accept the Victoria Cross from the King until March of that year.

Barker returns to Canada in May, 1919 as the most decorated Canadian of the war with a total of 12 medals. He is also mentioned in dispatches three times.

Those who flew with him say he was a very good flyer but an excellent marksman always modifying the guns of whatever plane he was in so that the sights were similar to those of the gun he loved to fire from horseback as a carefree boy back in Manitoba.

Part of the Snipe aircraft he was flying when he won the Victoria Cross is now on display at the Canadian War Museum in Ottawa alongside a plaque which states:

Lieutenant Colonel William G. Barker, one of the legendary aces of the war, remains the most decorated war hero in the history of Canadian military service.

A plaque on his tomb in the mausoleum of Toronto's Mount Pleasant Cemetery describes him as:

The most decorated war hero in the history of Canada, the British Empire and the Commonwealth of Nations.

Sadly, Barker continues to suffer from the effects of his wounds. His legs are permanently damaged and he can hardly move his left arm. He dies in 1930 at the age of 35 when he loses control of his plane during a demonstration flight at the RCAF Station Rockcliffe near Ottawa.

His funeral remains the largest National State Event in Toronto's history, attended by an honour guard of 2,000 soldiers. The cortege stretched for more than a mile and a half and was lined by more than 50,000 ordinary citizens paying their final respects.

CANADA 150

FROM TRAGEDY TO TRIUMPH

In this age of gender equality, hard to believe that it's not that long ago when the teaching of basic hygiene, domestic science and even sewing to school girls was considered too revolutionary to be allowed. It takes the tragic death of a 14 month old infant and his courageous mother to launch a revolution.

Adelaide Hoodless is devastated by the death of her 14 month old son Harold in the early 1900's. The diagnosis is something called "summer complaint", but Adelaide is convinced it has more to do with contaminated milk the boy was drinking. This is a time when pasteurization of milk is almost unheard of and most farmers and housewives know very little about basic hygiene. Adelaide becomes determined to provide women with the knowledge to prevent deaths such as that of her son.

She realizes that one of the best ways of teaching women, especially farm women, how to keep cleaner and safer homes and barns is to teach hygiene and what she calls domestic science in the classrooms of the nation. She firmly believes the highest possible vocation for a woman is to be a good homemaker and mother but she is aghast at the lack of training both boys and girls receive in schools.

"Boys", she says, "should have vocational training as well as learning the three R's and girls should learn how to properly care for a home, husband and children. Most of them", she says, "don't even understand basic hygiene".

Her beliefs are considered so revolutionary that even though her husband is Chairman of the Board of Education in Hamilton, she is banned from all classrooms in the City.

Undaunted, she begins a class in domestic science in the Hamilton YWCA with more than 100 women of all ages crowding in.

For ten years Adelaide travels Ontario, speaking about the importance of hygiene, cleanliness and frugality. She is credited with launching the National YWCA in Canada, writes a book urging vocational and domestic science, teaching in schools, then in 1897 founds the "Women's Institutes". Within a decade more than 500 Institute branches are opened in Canada.

Finally, after ten years of persuasion, the Ontario Government agrees to add domestic science and manual training to the school curricula. Adelaide is hired to write another book about homemaking and travels across the province explaining the new course.

She thus becomes the first woman on the Ontario Provincial payroll.

Adelaide Hoodless dies in the middle of a speech to the Federation of Women's Clubs in Massey Hall, Toronto.

Adelaide Hoodless is credited as the founder of the Women's Institutes, and co-founder of the National Council of Women, the Victorian Order of Nurses and the YWCA in Canada.

Another candidate surely to appear on Canadian currency!

THE REAL PATROIT

My listeners are enraged. We have just learned that our Federal Government will allow Colonel John McCrae's military medals to be sold to a non-Canadian! A Korean or perhaps an American collector will probably end up owning the medals awarded to the man who wrote, "In Flanders's Fields", probably the best known and best loved poem in the world.

The McCrae medals are going up for public auction and there is considerable interest around the world, except from the Government of Canada.

The Canadian War Museum is desperate to obtain the medals, which they deem to be among the most valuable Canadian military artifacts ever to become available on the open market. The Museum believes the medals will likely be sold for about $30,000, but they don't have nearly enough money to make a reasonable bid.

I contact Heritage Minister Sheila Copps. "Surely," I say, "Canada will not allow the McCrae medals to be sold out of the Country. They are among the most significant historical artifacts we have."

The call and the appeal on air are to no avail. The Government is not prepared to advance a single cent in order to keep the medals in Canada.

Within two days listeners to my show on CFRA Radio, Ottawa have donated not the $30,000 the Museum feels will be sufficient to buy the medals, but more than $80,000. All money is sent to a special fund we set up at the Museum.

How naïve we all are!

At the auction, the very first bid is for $100,000! As the bidding escalates well beyond $300,000 many of us are devastated, but lo and behold, just as the hammer comes down on a Korean bid for $350,000, a man no one knows anything about, holds up his hand.

"Four hundred thousand", he says quietly. "Sold", says the auctioneer.

We are stunned. Who is this man? Where is he from?

And then to our everlasting joy and gratitude we learn the good, no, make that great news.

The man who has just bought the Colonel John McCrae medals is a Toronto garment manufacturer named Arthur Lee, a man who came to Canada in 1969 as an immigrant.

He immediately donates the medals to the McCrae Museum in Guelph.

"I just wanted to show my love and gratitude to my adopted country," says Lee.

We offer to return the $80,000 to those who donated in our radio campaign, but not a single person asks for a refund. "Let the Museum keep the money to buy some other important artifacts" is the most frequent response. "Let's make sure that we do not break faith with those who die!"

THE DIVIDED CITY

You talk about bone-headed decisions! Few, if any, can top the bureaucrats who drew up the provincial boundaries between Saskatchewan and Alberta. Believe it or not in 1905, these mental giants declare the border to be right down the main street of Lloydminster and nothing, especially not common sense, is going to convince them to change their minds.

So for 25 years, Lloydminster, a community in the early days of no more than 2,000 people has two of everything. Two town councils, two fire brigades, two police forces and two separate provincial jurisdictions. As you can imagine, it drives everybody crazy to say nothing of the added cost.

Finally in 1930 the governments of the two provinces decide to stop the nonsense and declare Lloydminster to be one town under shared jurisdiction. The provinces reincorporate Lloydminster as a city in 1958.

But this by no means ends the confusion!

Since the border runs north and south right down the middle of 50th Avenue, all residents to the east of the Avenue are in Saskatchewan, while those living on the west side are in Alberta. Thus, not only does each side have different postal codes, but the Saskatchewan side has telephone area codes of 306 and 639—while just across the street the area codes are 780 and 587.

Another major problem rears its head when Saskatchewan refuses to adopt daylight saving time, while Alberta moves their clocks ahead and back, spring and fall. There is a rip roaring debate for several months but finally the Saskatchewan Government gives in and today in Lloydminster, everybody's watch is on Alberta daylight saving time.

Things really get hot and heavy for a while a few years ago when Saskatchewan legislates very stiff anti-smoking bylaws. You can puff away to your heart's content while riding a cab on the Alberta side, but when you cross 50th Avenue, presto—butt that smoke immediately buster or be busted.

Smoke filled pubs are jammed on the Alberta side, while pristine and half empty across the street.

You can imagine the screams of protest until finally, Alberta passes laws every bit as tough on smokers as those in Saskatchewan.

The one problem the government hasn't been able to solve is the rivalry over football.

You can guess what team they cheer for on the Saskatchewan side.

For sure not the same team they're cheering for just across the street!

THE MIRACLE OF THE MARSHES

Wild ducks would very well have gone the way of the passenger pigeon were it not for the work of an amazing little Canadian and thousands of volunteers.

In 1867, the year of Confederation, game officials estimate the wild duck population in North America at about 400 million. As we enter the 20th century it's less than half that. With modern farming destroying most of the bird's nesting grounds and virtually no laws regarding hunting, there is little doubt wild ducks are quickly headed for extinction.

When an organization called Ducks Unlimited is officially founded in 1937, there is hardly a wild duck to be seen anywhere on the continent.

Established by a group of interested sportsmen working voluntarily, the role of Ducks Unlimited today is exactly the same as it was the day it was launched--save waterfowl in North America and in particular save wild ducks from extinction.

The founders and volunteers today know that the key to success is the breeding and nesting grounds of the Canadian West. Save and create new marshes and sloughs and they will save the ducks.

They enlist, as their general manager, the perfect man for the job—Tom Main, a slender, wiry man of just five foot three, but packed with energy, dedication and talent.

In addition to being a skilled hydraulic engineer, Tom Main is a superb salesman. He recruits 2,000 volunteers in three provinces—"Key Men", he calls them, whose job is to persuade governments, groups and individuals to build dams and create marshes and wetlands of all kinds.

Tom persuades farmers that the success of their farming lies in the conservation of water resources. It's not long until most of the West is talking and thinking about duck conservation. Hundreds of dams, of all sizes are built, many by volunteers. In one project alone, 37,000 acres of marshland are restored.

Tom Main works tirelessly until gradually it beings to work! Ducks begin to reappear. New conservation and hunting laws are passed.

Today there are probably as many and perhaps more wild ducks on the North American continent as there were back the day old Sir John A. became our first prime minister.

They're still hard at it. You see Ducks Unlimited signs with their distinctive logo everywhere.

They call it "The miracle of the marshes"!

SNOWBLINDNESS AND COLD WAR INTRIGUE!

A case of snowblindness results in one of the great mineral discoveries of the 20th century and launches fascinating Cold War intrigue.

The year is 1930, prospector Gilbert LaBine and Charles St. Paul are prospecting along the shores of Great Bear Lake in the Northwest Territories looking for silver. At Echo Bay, St. Paul is stricken with snowblindness and can go no further. He urges LaBine to continue on without him, but LaBine refuses. It's the most momentous decision of his life.

LaBine stays with St. Paul, nursing his swollen eyes with tea leaves. As St. Paul recuperates, LaBine scouts the area. He stumbles upon something called cobalt bloom which almost invariably signifies silver.

There is silver there all right, but that's the least of his discovery, because, as he excitedly explores some more, he discovers a dark greenish-black substance rushing like a river in a zigzag course down the face of a rock.

It's pitchblende, the ore which is the only source of radium, one of the rarest minerals on earth and at that time one of the most valuable. When LaBine makes his discovery, the Belgian Congo is the only source of radium which in those days is used to make clock and watch faces glow in the dark and growing in the fight against some forms of cancer. It is valued in 1930 at $70,000 a gram and scientists estimate the world supply to be only 600 grams.

LaBine's find is the richest supply in the world, far larger than the Congo and makes him one of the richest men in the world. He calls the mine Eldorado.

Gold is also found in the Echo Bay area, so are silver, copper, iron and another mineral that is thought to have little value— uranium, which LaBine stockpiles in an abandoned mine.

As news spreads that exposure to radium is dangerous, demand drops along with the price and in 1940 LaBine closes the mine and allows it to flood.

What follows is a story of high drama, high stakes, subterfuge, secrecy and intrigue.

THE "BOMB"

Scientists in Nazi Germany have learned how to split a uranium atom. There are growing fears they may soon be able to make a weapon capable of unspeakable death and destruction. Enough firepower perhaps to win the war!

The Western Allies must beat them to it. We must create a nuclear bomb.

The Manhattan Project is born. Uranium is desperately needed.

"Canada we need you. We need your uranium but the Germans must not find out, nor the Japanese, and don't breathe a word of this to Stalin," are the instructions handed to the Canadian Government.

As luck would have it, Canadian Munitions and Supply Minister C.D. Howe knows Gilbert LaBine has stockpiled large amounts of uranium at the Eldorado Mine at Great Slave Lake in the Northwest Territories. The only problem is, the company now owning Eldorado is listed on the stock market, with thousands of shareholders.

Howe makes a deal with Labine. "Quietly buy up sufficient shares in the mine to take control. The Government of Canada will provide the money. The Government will then own the company, you can manage it but secrecy is of the utmost importance".

"But," some advisors say, "why doesn't the government just expropriate the mine under the War Measures Act and save ourselves a ton of money?"

"Because," replies the cagey Howe, "if we expropriate we will have to give the mine back to the shareholders after the war, but we will need that uranium long after this war is over!"

And so with the public totally unaware, the Government of Canada slowly acquires Eldorado mine stock while at the same time employing prospectors to try and find other deposits.

It is unclear how much money the Government spent buying up the shares and the subsequent costs involved in prospecting and shipping. Nor does it seem possible to obtain accurate figures concerning how much uranium Canada actually supplied to the Manhattan Project. Or if we ever received any payment. Most people don't think we were paid a cent. We will probably never know the truth.

We do know that the total cost of the Manhattan Project was in excess of $2 billion with more than 120,000 people employed.

Even today we are not fully aware of the extent of our role in developing the bomb but indications are we supplied the bulk of the vital uranium and a good portion of that came from the Eldorado mine thanks to Gilbert LaBine's decision to stockpile what he thought was a worthless mineral!

THE BRAVEST OF THEM ALL!

One hundred and seventy-eight Canadians were cited for conspicuous courage in action during the disastrous Dieppe Raid, August 19, 1942. The bravest of them all was Victoria Cross winner Colonel Charles Merritt.

From their point of landing on the Dieppe Beach, Colonel Merritt's unit has to advance across a bridge in the nearby village of Pourville. The bridge is a death trap, being swept by heavy machinegun, mortar and artillery fire. Of the first groups of men who try the crossing, very few live! The roadway is covered with bodies; the Canadians are pinned down, unable to advance across the bridge and cut off from retreating to the beach.

Colonel Merritt rushes forward and raising his helmet over his head shouts, "Forward, follow me, there's nothing to worry about."

The survivors quickly follow him across. Merritt then leads several rushes at enemy pillboxes, single-handedly destroying at least one by dashing forward through heavy fire and lobbing in hand grenades.

He's hit once, staggers back to his feet, is hit again but keeps urging his men forward. When several of his runners are killed or wounded, he dashes through a hail of bullets to direct his unit's operations.

When ordered to withdraw he stalks a sniper who has killed several of his men and with a hand grenade silences him.

His men are ordered to withdraw to the beach where ships are assembled to rescue the few who survive. Colonel Merritt remains behind, collecting Bren (light weight machine guns) and Tommy guns to prepare his defensive position.

From it he successfully covers the withdrawal from the beach until he is taken prisoner.

Merritt is sent to Prison Camp Oflag V11-B in Bavaria. Together with 64 others he escapes through a 120 foot tunnel during the night of June 4, 1943. All are recaptured.

This citation of his Victoria Cross concludes:

"To this commanding officer's personal daring, the success of his unit's operations and the safe re-embarkation of a large portion of it were chiefly due."

Of the 4,963 Canadian soldiers who hit the Dieppe beach, only 2,210 return to England, many of them wounded.

In just a few terrible hours, 916 young Canadians are killed, 1,946 taken prisoner.

Those who were there agree the death toll would have been even higher were it not for the incredible bravery of Colonel Charles Merritt.

He died in Vancouver on July 12, 2000 at the age of 91, after serving for four years as a Federal Member of Parliament.

WE BEAT THE YANKS

The Americans may claim the honour, but it was a Canadian built ship that really ushers in the age of steam.

It's a historical fact. The first ship ever to cross the Atlantic Ocean using only steam power is the Royal William, a wooden paddlewheeler launched at Quebec City in April of 1831. It was that trip and the resulting publicity that convinced the ship building industry to abandon sails and install steam engines.

Built entirely in Canada, the Royal William is 182 feet long, weighs 1,370 tons gross, has engines that develop 300 horsepower and has a top speed of about eight knots. Until 1837 she is the largest passenger ship in the world!

She's built to run between Quebec City and Halifax and makes three such runs, but the cholera epidemic of 1832 discourages travel and the service has to be abandoned. The Royal William is then sold to a Boston company and when she steams into Boston Harbor in June, 1833, history is made when she becomes the first British steamship ever to enter an American port.

Later that year the Royal William is sent to England for sale and again, history is made. She leaves Pictou, Nova Scotia on August 18, 1833 and 20 days later reaches England to great fanfare and international press coverage.

At first the claim is that the Royal William is the first vessel to cross the Atlantic under continuous steam. This isn't very accurate however, since they had to stop the engines every fourth day to clear her boilers of salt. The condenser which made uninterrupted steaming possible wasn't invented until the following year, but the Royal William did steam the entire way unlike the American built ship the Savannah, which crossed the Atlantic in 1819.

It is true the Savannah was a steamship, but she used her sails for most of that trip.

But the Royal William's history making isn't over. She eventually ends up in the Spanish Navy and incredibly, becomes the first steamship in the world to fire her guns in anger during a minor Spanish rebellion.

Next time you are in Halifax be sure to visit the Maritime Museum of the Atlantic where a large wooden model of the Royal William is on display.

DANGEROUS MONEY

The crowd at a Montreal baseball game cheers the news that Canada's richest man has died. It is a sentiment widely held across the Country!

His name is Sir Herbert Samuel Holt, a native of Dublin who comes to Canada at an early age to earn his fortune. And what a fortune he makes.

He starts out as an engineer on the staff of several railways, becoming superintendent of construction for the CPR. After making a pile of money laying tracks through Northern Ontario and in the Calgary and Edmonton areas, Holt turns to energy development, creating Montreal Light and Power and what later becomes Quebec Hydro.

Turning to banking he becomes President of the Royal Bank of Canada from 1908 until 1934 and Chairman of the Board until his death in 1941.

His assets during the Great Depression years are estimated at $3 billion, making him by far the richest man in Canada and also by far the most hated.

While his and all other banks are foreclosing on mortgages and kicking people out of their homes across the Country, Holt has nothing but disdain for the suffering.

One of his more famous quotes is:

"If I am rich and powerful, while you are suffering the stranglehold of poverty and the humiliation of social assistance; if I was able, at

the peak of the Depression, to make 150% profits each year, it is foolishness on your part not to do likewise and for me, it is the fruit of wise administration!"

You can imagine what kind of reaction that creates!

Holt's life is threatened several times.

For several years, during the "Dirty 30's" Sir Herbert Samuel Holt, richest man in Canada one of the richest men in the world, is virtually a captive in his own home, afraid to leave except under heavy guard at all times.

As he walks to work every day in downtown Montreal he is guarded by four armed men. Two in front, two behind.

For the Montreal Royals Baseball team, 1941 is a banner year. Although the club finished second during the season, on September 29 they are on the threshold of defeating the Newark Bears for the International League Championship.

More than 20,000 jam into Delormier Stadium ready to celebrate. Suddenly, for no apparent reason, the crowd bursts into loud cheering and clapping. The players look up in surprise.

There's the news, being spelled out on the scoreboard.

Sir Herbert Samuel Holt has died!

CANADA 150

THE KIDNAPPING

Stop the presses! One of Canada's most famous brewers has just been kidnapped!

It's a hot summer day in 1934, John S. Labatt is driving on a lonely country road not far from London, Ontario. A roadblock halts his car. Three masked men force Labatt, President of the world famous Labatt Brewing Company, out of his vehicle.

Labatt is bound and gagged and taken to a summer cottage in the Muskoka Lakes area where he is chained to a bed. Labatt is forced to write a note to his brother Hugh begging him to pay $150,000 ransom money. (Worth about $2.5 million today).

On the back of the note a man who signs himself "three fingered Abe" tells Hugh to go the Royal York Hotel in Toronto to await instructions. The note is placed in Labatt's car and driven to London with Hugh receiving a phone call telling him where the vehicle can be found.

The story is flashed around the globe. Reporters from as far away as England and France rush for Canada. Every Canadian newspaper blazons the story across the front page. Police leaves are cancelled and known criminals are hauled off the streets for questioning.

The publicity is matched only by the Lindbergh kidnapping.

At the Royal York, Hugh is paged and a phone caller tells him to drop the $150,000 at the Humber River Bridge.

But before this can happen, the kidnappers, worried over the intense media coverage, decide to set their hostage free. They tape Labatt's eyes, drive him to the north end of Toronto and give him a dollar of the one hundred dollars they stole from him. "Get a cab home," he's instructed.

One of the kidnappers flees to the United States where he dies in a gang shootout. Three others are caught and sentenced to long prison terms, but the strange story doesn't end there.

One of those jailed is a small town gambler from Kentucky named David Meisner. During the trial John Labatt looks Meisner in the eye and proclaims, "Yes that's the man. I would recognize him anywhere as the man who kidnapped me".

But after 13 months in jail Meisner is set free when another man confesses to the crime. Meisner sues Labatt and wins $5,500. (Worth about $95,000 today).

The whole affair shakes Labatt very badly. He becomes a recluse and while continuing on as head of Labatt Brewing for a number of years, he is seldom ever again seen in public.

THE COMPASSION HOTEL

Canada's first female senator often fills her home with so many refugees and homeless immigrants there is scarcely room for her own family.

By the time Cairine Wilson is appointed to the Senate in 1930 she is already deeply involved in fighting for women's rights and those of minorities. Prime Minister William Lyon Mackenzie King is so impressed, he appoints her as Canada's first female Senator only four months after women are deemed to be legally persons and thus allowed into the Red Chamber.

Her voice is heard loudly and clearly on many issues.

As President of the League of Nations Society of Canada in 1938 Cairine Wilson speaks out forcefully against the Munich Agreement's appeasement of Hitler.

The King Government refuses to allow Jews fleeing Germany into Canada, but Cairine, working behind the scenes, manages to arrange the acceptance of 100 Jewish orphans and argues passionately to open our doors to more.

She is one of very few in the Country to publicly oppose the confiscation of Japanese Canadians' property and their incarceration following Pearl Harbor.

As Chairman of the Senate Labour and Immigration Committee during the immediate postwar years, the demands upon her compassion are often overwhelming.

She simply could not say no to those in distress and for several years you can hardly move in her spectacular and luxurious Ottawa home; every guest and spare room are filled with displaced persons. Neighbours call it "Compassion Hotel"!

She wins the hearts of everyone in the Country, no matter what political affiliation and in 1950 is chosen "Woman of the Year"; in addition she is one of the first women ever to be awarded the French Legion of Honour for her work on behalf of French refugee children.

Cairine Wilson becomes the first woman to hold the position of Senate speaker and is appointed to the University of Ottawa's Board of Regents in 1960. An Ottawa high school bears her name.

If you visit the Senate Chambers today you will see a statue of Senator Wilson just below the plaque at the main entrance.

THE BEST DAMN
SATELLITE IN SPACE!

The Russians started it. Sputnik! Remember peering into the
night sky trying to spot the star that's moving across the horizon?
Great excitement. A satellite circling the planet in 1957! Who
could imagine such a thing? What's next!

Well, what's next is panic from the West and a frantic race to
catch up in the space race with the dreaded Ruskies! After all, this
is the middle of the Cold War and the idea of being blasted from
outer space sends shivers down our spines. Diefenbunkers spring
up (or down) across Canada.

The United States launches Explorer 1 a few months later and
invites Canada to build a satellite. "You build it, we'll rocket it
into space," they tell us.

The scientists and engineers at the Defence Research
Telecommunications Establishment at Shirley's Bay just west
of Ottawa, design and manufacture one of the most successful
satellites ever sent into orbit.

Launched from Vandenberg Air Force Base in California,
September 29, 1962, Alouette 1 is designed to examine the
ionosphere from above, something vital for the defence of
North America.

We know that the Soviets have dozens, maybe hundreds of
nuclear tipped missiles aimed at us. Our only chance of defending
ourselves is to spot them coming in early enough to fire off a few
of our own and maybe get our children under their school desks
and officials into the Diefenbunkers.

A system of early warning stations is built across Canada's
far north (The DEW line). If an incoming missile is

detected the information will immediately be radioed back to defence headquarters buried deep inside an American mountain somewhere.

High frequency (HF) radio is the primary means of communication over long distances in those days but HF radio depends upon reflections from the ionosphere. Especially in the far north, the radio waves can be affected by electrical impulses from the Northern Lights. All the early warning systems in the world will be of little use if radio communications are disrupted. It's something they didn't tell us in those days, but it scares the pants off those in the know.

The problem is that only the bottom of the ionosphere can be investigated. What is desperately needed to improve the communication system is data from the top side of the ionosphere.

That's the job of Alouette 1, provide data from the top of the ionosphere. And what a great job it does!

Designed for only a one year lifespan, Alouette 1 is decommissioned, while still functioning perfectly, ten years later. Until the 1970's it is the satellite that provides information for more scientific publications than any other satellite in space.

It is acknowledged today as one of the most successful scientific satellites ever built or, as one of the scientists who help build it told me, "It is the best damn satellite ever built period!"

The Institute of Electrical and Electronic Engineers has designated Alouette 1 as one of the ten most outstanding achievements of the first 100 years of engineering in Canada and recognized the satellite as an "International Milestone of Electrical Engineering".

Alouette 1 is still up there and according to those who should know could probably be turned on tomorrow and work perfectly again.

Mine is the only live broadcast of that historic launch with the recording available at the National Archives.

FORGOTTEN HEROES

Patton, Briggs and Prentice. Three names you've probably never heard of, but they are Canadian heroes, largely forgotten except by their families and those whose lives they saved.

The first George Medal for extreme bravery in a non-combat situation is awarded to Lieutenant John Patton of Hamilton, Ontario, who, during a bombing raid on London, England, hitches a cable to an unexploded bomb and hauls it from a heavily populated area to a vacant field. He risks his life every inch of the way since the bomb could easily have detonated at the slightest bump or jar. His act saves many lives.

Lieutenant Commander W.E.F. Briggs of Vancouver, while Commander of the corvette "Orillia'" saves the lives of 95 men, rescued from British ships torpedoed in the Atlantic. On another occasion Briggs safely tows through mountainous seas, a heavily damaged British tanker with a million dollar cargo of desperately needed oil. He then later rescues 30 crew members of a torpedoed lumber ship. For his exploits, Lieutenant Commander Briggs is awarded the Distinguished Service Cross.

Commander James Douglas "Chummy" Prentice of Halifax also wins the Distinguished Service Cross for the manner in which he commands his ship H.M.C.S Chambly. The Chambly becomes the first Canadian corvette to capture a Nazi submarine.

Prentice discovers the sub lying in ambush ahead of a convoy. Depth charges force the sub to surface. A running gun battle ensues, during which Prentice manages to skilfully elude several torpedoes. It finally ends with the surrender of the German craft.

In the official Citation, Commander Prentice's conduct is described as:

"Marked by the utmost skill, coolness and efficiency".

The Chambly, with Prentice in command, is credited with taking part in the sinking of at least two other enemy submarines.

THE GUARD

Not all acts of heroism and bravery are performed on the battlefield during times of war. There isn't a soldier anywhere braver than a little French Canadian girl who risked her life rather than desert her post.

It's September 1941 and the Allies are in desperate need of equipment and munitions. A forest fire breaks out near a shell-filling plant in central Quebec. High winds drive the flames towards the plant.

As embers begin floating down, dangerously near the gunpowder, all employees are ordered to evacuate.

Everyone leaves except for Rita Foucault. It is Rita's job to guard vital equipment at the plant. She refuses to leave. "I cannot allow this equipment to remain unguarded," she says. "My job is to guard and guard it I will."

All night she remains at her post as the fire draws ever nearer. All lights go out as hydro poles catch fire. Live sparks fly past on the wind, a single one of which could easily blow the entire plant into smithereens, but Rita calmly remains at her post.

At the last minute the wind changes, the plant is saved.

Rita Foucault continues her work with hardly any official recognition, just one of countless acts of self-sacrifice, bravery and outright heroism that became commonplace on the home front during those dark days when the jackboots never seem to stop their marching.

CANADA 150

BANISHED

This is the forest primeval. The murmuring pines and the hemlocks,
Bearded with moss, and in garments green, indistinct in the twilight,
Stand like Druids of eld, with voices sad and prophetic,
Stand like harpers hoar, with beards that rest on their bosoms.
Loud from its rocky caverns, the deep-voiced neighboring ocean.
Speaks, and in accents disconsolate answers the wail of the forest.

This is the forest primeval, but where are the hearts that beneath it
Leaped like the roe, when hears in the woodland the voice of the
huntsman?
Where is the thatch-roofed village, the home of Acadian farmers,
Men whose lives glided on like rivers that water the woodlands,
Darkened by shadows of earth, but reflecting an image of heaven?
Waste are those pleasant farms, and the farmers forever departed!
Scattered like dust and leaves, when the mighty blasts of October
Seize them, and whirl them aloft, and sprinkle them far o'er the ocean.

Naught but tradition remains of the beautiful village of Grand-Pré.

Ye who believe in affection that hopes, and endures, and is patient,
Ye who believe in the beauty and strength of women's devotion,
List to the mournful tradition, still sung by the pines of the forest;
List to a tale of love in Acadie, home of the happy.

The first three verses of one of the longest and most sorrowful
poems ever written—Henry Wadsworth Longfellow's famous
Evangeline, a soulful lament to the expulsion from Nova Scotia
of about 12,000 Acadians, mostly French Canadians and Metis.

Some of those banished from their homes for refusing to swear allegiance to the British King ended up in Louisiana where today, known as Cajuns, they have developed a lively and distinct culture and language.

What isn't as widely known is that about 1,400 of the Acadians somehow managed to escape to Prince Edward Island, then known as Ile St. Jean. There they lived peacefully until the French had to surrender to the British their last bastion in "New France", the massive fort at Louisburg. This convinced France to end the Seven Years War with Britain and sign a treaty essentially handing over what is now Canada to the British. (The Paris Treaty, 1763).

Sadly the Treaty provided no protection for the Acadians of Ile St. Jean who were almost immediately ordered deported.

Nine transport ships carrying about 1,200 heartbroken Acadians sailed from Port La Joye. (Across the harbour from Charlottetown).

No poet has ever eulogized their desperate plight, but one of the eye witnesses, George Hart paints the picture very well in his diary:

"Ile St. Jean was the scene of sorrow. The drooping shoulders and gloomy countenances of the men, the tears and cries of women and children. All roads were soon crowded with carts filled high with the few belongings of the weary, broken-hearted people plodding alongside."

The tragedy had only just begun. The nine ships were soon scattered by a terrible storm. Two were lost at sea with 700 innocent souls aboard. Some escaped to Quebec and St. Pierre and Miquelon still owned by France.

Thirty families took refuge in the woods near Malpeque and actually stayed in hiding for several years.

Of the more than 14,000 Acadians who settled Atlantic Canada it is estimated that fewer than 500 were left after the expulsions.

One of the saddest chapters in Canada's history.

THE PADDLER!

This Country was opened up by the greatest paddlers and oarsmen the world has ever seen; so it's only fitting that the first world championship Canada ever won was for rowing.

Our first sports hero is a Toronto boy, Edward Hanlon, who gets his start rowing boats near his home where Toronto Harbour is now.

Hanlon becomes amateur champion oarsman of Toronto Bay at the age of 18, then just three years later decides to make a bit of money and turns professional.

In those days rowing is a much more popular sport than it is today; in fact it was just about the only professional sport in the Country, so when Hanlon defeats all competitors in the Philadelphia Races during his first professional year, he is hailed as a great hero in his homeland.

The next year, Hanlon goes on to win the Canadian Championship, then the American Championship and within two years has set the world record for the famous race on the River Tyne.

It's in 1880 that Edward Hanlon becomes the first Canadian to win a World Championship at any sport, beating the best the world has to offer in the four and a half mile race up the River Thames.

He holds this crown for four straight years.

Hanlon wins more than 150 races in his career, winning more than $50,000, an awful lot of money in those days when you can buy a beautiful three bedroom home for less than $5,000 and the average yearly wage is $432!

He's recognized for many years as Canada's number one sports hero.

Those who know say he has never been surpassed in skill, style, or heart!

MARILYN BELL

Marilyn Bell! Who's Marilyn Bell? Why would we be interested in having some 16 year old kid no one has ever heard of swim the lake for us?

We don't know their exact words, but officials of the Canadian National Exhibition in Toronto (the CNE) aren't the least bit interested in having 16 year old Marilyn take part in promoting the CNE by swimming across Lake Ontario. They want world famous American long-distance swimmer Florence Chadwick to become the first person to swim the 32 miles across the Lake as a great publicity stunt for their annual exhibition.

In fact, they want Chadwick so badly they offer her $10,000 if she can swim from Youngstown, New York to the CNE grounds in Toronto where they hope large crowds will gather to greet her.

Since the CNE is a Canadian exhibition the question arises, why restrict the marathon to just one American? Why not open it up to everyone and hopefully some Canadians, in particular this 16 year old kid named Marilyn Bell, might give it a try.

At first, the officials are scornful, not believing that any Canadian could swim the 32 miles in the September cold, especially not a 16 year old girl, besides which, they believe that Chadwick, being a major celebrity, will attract far more attention than some unknown Canadian kid.

But in the end, a grudging agreement is reached that allows Marilyn Bell and another Toronto swimmer named Winnie

Roach to get in the water with Chadwick, but the $10,000 is for Chadwick alone. Bell says she is doing it, not for money, but for Canada!

At exactly 11:07 p.m., September 8, 1954, 16 year old Marilyn Bell enters the cold water of Lake Ontario at Youngstown, New York, alongside Florence Chadwick and Winnie Roach. All the media attention is on Chadwick.

When it comes to courage and endurance there are few feats in history which come close to comparing to what that 16 year old Canadian girl endured.

During that first night, waves peak at nearly 15 feet, blood sucking eels clamp to her body, the cold is numbing, and she fights nausea and severe cramps. Her trainer, Gus Ryder, extends corn syrup on a stick for nourishment, then liniment to rub on her pain wracked limbs. She's in agony from a strained tendon in her ankle.

By late afternoon the next day she's all alone in the water. Florence Chadwick was hauled out of the Lake at 6 a.m., suffering cramps and fatigue. Winnie Roach lasted a bit longer, but she also had to finally give up.

Marilyn bravely swims on but suddenly appears to fall into unconsciousness. Lifeboats rush out. Her friend Joan Cooke, in bloomers and bra, jumps into the water and swims alongside her. Marilyn revives.

By dusk she stops swimming and turns a tear-streaked face to the accompanying boat and begs to come out. Her father, worried for her health, orders her out of the water. Ignoring him, Gus Ryder holds up a blackboard with a chalk message reading, "If you quit—I quit".

Marilyn thinks of the handicapped pupils who have gained so much from their swimming instructions and goes on. Radio stations broadcast hourly bulletins on her position. Newspapers issue special editions. The nation is galvanized by the idea of a little 16 year old girl all alone out there in that huge cold lake!

She is only semi-conscious when, 20 hours and 59 minutes after setting out from Youngstown, she finally staggers out of the water, oblivious to the estimated 250,000 people who have flocked to an area just west of the CNE grounds. The cheering as she staggers from the water can be heard blocks away.

The CNE decides to give her the $10,000 which she donates to the swim classes for handicapped children she is involved with. She's named newsmaker of the year by the Canadian Press, awarded the Lou Marsh Trophy as Canada's Athlete of the Year, is inducted into Canada's Sports Hall of Fame, the Canadian Swimming Hall of Fame and is named one of Canada's top athletes of the century.

In addition, the National Historic Sites and Monuments Board has designated Bell's crossing of Lake Ontario a National Historic Event and a federal plaque was erected in 2008 near the site of her landfall.

The year after her historic Lake swim, Marilyn Bell becomes the youngest person to swim across the English Channel.

The latest news is that as she approaches the age of 80, Marilyn Bell, now Marilyn Bell Lasico still enjoys swimming, but now only in backyard pools!

CANADA 150

THE RAYMORE DRIVE DISASTER

Thirty-five people die on Toronto's Raymore Drive the terrible stormy night of October 15, 1954, swept away by the rampaging Humber River. A little footbridge is blamed.

Hurricane Hazel should not have struck a surprised and unprepared Toronto. After all, it had raged through the Caribbean and across the eastern United States for ten days with winds up to 130 miles per hour. It had already claimed as many as 1,000 lives before crossing Lake Ontario and taking dead aim at Toronto.

The thinking was that the storm would lose a lot of strength crossing the Allegheny Mountains, so when rain began to fall on Toronto late on the afternoon of October 15, only a few people were worried.

What those few seemed to realize was that when the flagging hurricane hit the cold front that had been stationary over Southern Ontario for several days, the "perfect storm" would result, creating the worst natural disaster in the history of Toronto.

There had been heavy rainfall in the Toronto area prior to Hazel, so the ground was already soaked and to complicate things, hurricanes this far north were almost unheard of. Hurricanes, most Canadians believed, were a problem in the tropics not up here in the north! No evacuations were ordered.

How wrong we were. Suddenly the wind-whipped rain becomes

almost blinding. Creeks and rivers begin to flood, more than 50 bridges, and many parts of important highways as well as railways are washed away.

The Humber River flowing through Toronto becomes a raging torrent, 20 feet above its normal level.

Then disaster strikes. A small footbridge across the Humber begins tearing apart. A section is swept away, but unfortunately a part of it remains attached to shore re-directing the flood waters directly onto a quiet little residential street called Raymore Drive. Within minutes, some say seconds, entire houses are swept away.

Some residents are able to escape by wading through nose deep water but many cannot withstand the incredible force of the angry, roiling water.

By morning, 14 houses have disappeared from Raymore Drive. Of the 81 people killed in Canada by Hurricane Hazel, 35 of them die on Raymore Drive.

The most tragic is at 148 Raymore, where nine members of the Edwards and Neil families succumb to the raging waters, three adults and six children. The bodies of two year old Frank and three month old John Edwards are never found.

THE KISSING BRIDGES

Today there's opposition to pipelines but it's not that long ago, when, believe it or no, the opposition came from those opposed to covered bridges!

Fully aware that it is the custom for young ladies to be kissed when crossing a covered bridge, more than a few pulpits shake with fiery sermons warning that covered bridges will lead young people into immorality.

Thus when the decision is made to cover the Hartland Bridge that spans the Saint John River between Hartland and Somerville, New Brunswick, the opposition is heated, not all of it from the clergy.

"Covered bridges are a pathway to hell," shouts one man at a public meeting. "My children will never enter a covered bridge; those bridges are immoral," claims another.

There was no such opposition when the bridge was first built (uncovered) just as we entered the 20th century. For good reason. Until the bridge the only means of crossing the River between Hartland and Somerville was by ferry, slow and costly. So when the uncovered bridge is officially opened on July 4, 1901, a joyful crowd of more than 2,000 are there to applaud.

Actually the first person to cross the bridge is the local doctor responding to an emergency a few days prior to the official opening Since the floor of the structure was not yet completed, workers laid down some planks for the good doctor to make his way safely across.

The problem was that uncovered wooden bridges usually last only about 15 to 20 years and by 1922 the Hartland Bridge is badly in need of repair. So despite the opposition, the decision is made to cover it and greatly prolong its life.

So in 1922 the Hartland Bridge at 1,282 feet becomes the longest covered bridge in the world and today is a National Historic Site.

Only three provinces still have covered bridges. There are many in New Brunswick, a handful in Quebec and one in Ontario, the West Montrose Bridge (Kissing Bridge) near Waterloo, also a National Historic Site.

Today you can kiss all you like while crossing any of the covered bridges, but despite the fact the Hartland Bridge is part of the Trans-Canada Highway you had better not exceed 30 kilometres an hour or they'll give you a nice little memento that's a long way from a kiss!

THE GARDENS

Toronto's Maple Leaf Gardens is one of Canada's finest monuments to cooperation between labour and management.

It's 1930 and the financial world is in shock. The "Dirty 30's" lie just ahead, but in the midst of all this, Conn Smythe is trying to raise $1.5 million to build what he calls Maple Leaf Gardens. It is to be a new home for Smythe's newly acquired hockey team he names the Maple Leafs.

Even hockey stars like Ace Bailey are going door to door, trying to sell stock in the project. Thousands of dollars' worth is bought, the site in downtown Toronto is purchased, but financial conditions worsen. Some of those who invested awake to find they are broke as the stock market crashes.

Things look grim and the Board of Directors decides to wait a year or two before proceeding. Smythe fears it will spell the end of the arena and perhaps even the Maple Leafs hockey team.

Then, Frank Selke, an assistant to Smythe and later to become one of hockey's ablest administrators, has a brainwave.

An electrician by trade, Selke is still a member of the International Brotherhood of Electrical Workers. He rushes to a nearby building where the business managers of local trade unions are holding a meeting.

Bursting in, Selke, a fantastic salesman, manages to convince them to work for 80 per cent of their regular wages and accept the other 20 per cent in Maple Leaf Gardens stock.

Selke tells them if the arena project collapses, confidence in the building trades will be greatly affected. He manages to convince them.

Rushing back to Smythe's directors' meeting, he informs them of the unions' agreement. So impressed by this are the directors that many of them decide to proceed immediately with the arena, and five months later, November 12th, 1931, the Maple Leafs and the Chicago Black Hawks meet for the first game ever in "state of the art" Maple Leaf Gardens.

The rest, as they say is history, except that many of those tradesmen who agreed to take Gardens' stock instead of wages became very rich people. Very rich!

BUMPING INTO
BENJAMIN FRANKLIN

When young Fleury Mesplet meets Benjamin Franklin in London during the 18th century neither one has any idea the role the chance encounter will play in the lives of Canadians.

Mesplet, sensing the growing frustration and anger that a few years later lead to the bloody French Revolution, packs up his printing business in Lyon and sets up shop in London.

Franklin, a leading publisher and author from Philadelphia is in London as a special envoy from the 13 American colonies trying to calm the waters between Britain and its raw but burgeoning North American possessions.

How the two meet isn't clear but they do, and Franklin takes a liking to the young Frenchman, eventually persuading him to come to Philadelphia to start a print shop.

Aided by a letter of introduction from Franklin, Mesplet immigrates to the colony and quickly becomes a leading citizen of that community.

When the American Revolution breaks out, Canada is attacked by the rebels and for about a year Montreal is peacefully captured and occupied.

As luck would have it, Franklin is appointed to head a special commission sent to Montreal to try and convince those north of the St. Lawrence River and the Great Lakes to join the rebellion.

Mesplet accompanies him as the official Commission Printer.

As history records, the British kick the Americans out of Montreal, but for some reason Mesplet, perhaps feeling at home in the French milieu, decides to stay, and although imprisoned for a while, is soon allowed to take the oath of allegiance to the King and sets up his presses in what is now "Old Montreal". He thus becomes the first printer in that City, and on June 1778 publishes the first issue of "La Gazette du Commerce et Litteraire", making it today one of the oldest newspapers in North America.

Mesplet and his editor are imprisoned for three years for their abuse of local judges but upon release start publishing again, first in French only then in the late 1700's bilingual, finally switching to English only in 1882. The Montreal Gazette is today one of only two English language daily newspapers left in all of Quebec, the other is the Sherbrooke Record.

As for Benjamin Franklin—well that's a different story—you can see him on any American 100 dollar bill!

PIRATES OF THE
THOUSAND ISLANDS

These are pirates with a difference all right, but pirates nonetheless. And cruel enough, since on more than one occasion they remove fingers from victims who aren't yanking off their rings and handing them over quickly enough.

The pirates led by William (Bill) Johnson, don't have heavily armed warships, sloops or schooners; their attack vessel is an eight man rowboat made especially for them by one of the shipwrights in either Alexandria Bay or what is now Clayton, New York.

It's perfect for pirating amidst the countless narrow channels and hidden coves of the Thousand Islands. Eight men rowing is faster than anything else on the water, including steamboats.

Since their victims are always Canadian, and the Americans are still chafing at their loss during the war of 1812, Johnson becomes a great hero on the U.S. side. So much so that even today, as just one example, every August the tourist town of Alexandria Bay, New York holds an annual ten day festival called Bill Johnson's Pirate Days, complete with pretend sword fights and pirate attacks.

During his pirate days the Americans pay lip service to arresting Johnson but do nothing but look the other way and sometimes even break into applause at his every appearance on the New York side.

That is until Bill Johnson and his pirates attack, set afire and sink the Sir Robert Peel steamship just in front of Alexandria Bay.

The Sir Robert Peel is a pretty fancy ship by the standards of the day; big at 160 feet long, 30 feet wide, powered by two paddlewheels.

It's a warm May evening in 1838 when she sets out from Prescott with 19 well-heeled passengers and a load of freight, bound for Toronto.

She needs wood for her boilers so pulls into a wharf on the south side of Wellesley Island in the heart of the Thousand Islands just upstream of Alexandria Bay where men begin to pile cordwood into her hold.

Suddenly, out of the dark, rush Johnson and eight of his fellow pirates, dressed as Indians. They order the passengers and crew off the ship, some of them in their night clothes, and take command.

Johnson later claims he intended to capture the ship and use her to supply a group of Americans who plan to attack Canada, but that's not the way it works out.

Neither Johnson, nor anyone else in the attack party, knows anything about operating a steam ship. The plan is to have several knowledgeable seamen meet them immediately after the attack and they will take over running the vessel.

For some reason, probably because they are too drunk, the seamen never show up.

There are several versions of this, but most seem to agree that the pirates discover a cache of champagne in the Sir Robert Peel's dining room and by the time they have finished "sampling", things get out of control.

The ship is set afire, pushed away from the Island and drifts down the St. Lawrence until it sinks only a few feet off shore from Alexandria Bay, where the wreck remains today, a favourite site for scuba divers.

The Americans finally arrest Johnson and his men, but when the pirates go on trial a jury can't be found to convict them of anything, so they all go free.

Johnson's pirate days are over, but he basks in fame, sometimes attending the many plays staged about him. He ends his days as the lighthouse keeper at the Rock Island Light not far from where he and his pirate band dressed as Indians, carried out the most famous pirate attack in Canadian history!

DISASTER!

No greater disaster has ever befallen Canadian fishermen than the Great American Gale!

It's the morning of Friday, October 4, 1851, the sea off the north coast of Prince Edward Island is as calm as innocence asleep. More than 100 schooners, all sails set, are standing in close to the Island, their captains expecting to catch their fish in the shallow water.

Gradually, during the day, the brilliant sunshine turns to grey and towards evening, the wind picks up. About 4 p.m., the fleet becomes worried and sets sail. It's too late!

The storm strikes with terrible fury. By next morning the sea is convulsive, the beaches a seething mass of foam. The winds shift several times.

All day Saturday, the storm continues unabated, well into Saturday night. Not until Sunday evening does the wind begin to die.

The toll is terrible. On the Cavendish shore one of the wrecks can be seen by those on the beach, 13 men are lashed to the rigging almost naked from the force of the wind. All are dead.

Another wreck washes up on shore. Townsmen rush to her, but the entire crew is drowned. In an adjoining cove, 14 men have lashed several casks together to form a raft, only four of them survive.

At Rustico, the loss of life is shocking and not just among Canadians. One New Englander loses four sons and a nephew.

By Monday, 80 wrecks lie between East Point and North Cape containing about 150 drowned men. Many other ships and men are lost far out at sea.

Islanders flock to the shores in an effort to save those they can. Islander homes are opened to survivors. Island graveyards provide the last resting place for many unknown mariners. Wrecks litter Island beaches well into the 20th century.

There are many acts of heroism and the News of Gloucester, newspaper of the most important fishing town in New England at the time, pays tribute to the manner in which the Islanders risked their lives to save American sailors and for their hospitality to the survivors.

It is considered to be the worst maritime disaster in the history of Prince Edward Island.

THE WEBSITE

It's true. You can now buy t-shirts, coffee mugs, mousepads, tote bags, baseball caps and sweat pants in recognition of one of the most brutal murders in Canada's history. Five murders as a matter of fact, that have their own website!

Mind you, books have been written, movies made, plays staged about those murders so we shouldn't be surprised that they now have their own website.

We're talking of course about the Donnelly murders or the Black Donnellys as they were known in and around their home town of Lucan just north of London, Ontario.

The feuding may have started back in Ireland, but there is no question that when they immigrated to Canada, some of the Donnellys were troublemakers, constantly quarrelling with neighbours to the point where it seemed that anything that went wrong in the Lucan area was automatically attributed to the "Black Donnellys".

It culminates shortly after midnight February 4, 1880 when a swarm of men pour into the Donnelly house. James Donnelly and his wife Johannah are the first to die. A visiting niece, Bridget, is dragged out from her hiding place behind a laundry basket and killed.

A son, Tom, gives the murderers the most trouble. He breaks away at one point and runs outside, but is overcome and killed with a shovel.

Incredibly, all this time, a neighbour's boy, Johnny O'Connor is hiding under a bed. When the killers finally leave, he dashes to the nearest farm and later appears as a witness in the court case.

The mob's dirty work isn't over yet though.

They set fire to the Donnelly house, then make their way to Will Donnelly's home, another son, about three miles away.

There they kill John Donnelly in the mistaken belief he is Will.

Everyone in the area knows very well who the killers are, but no one is willing to provide sufficient evidence for a conviction.

Despite the fact that Johnny O'Connor and others provide eye witness accounts of the murders and identify some of the killers, no one is ever convicted in what may be the worst murderous rampage this Country has ever seen.

The worst or not, as we can see from the books, plays, movies, and now websites and souvenirs, it certainly is the most celebrated!

By the way, just added to the Donnelly website—children's bibs saying "I Love the Donnellys!"

CANADA 150

BLOODY DECEMBER

"The bloody Limeys trained us to die", my stepfather Bert Whetter insisted this until the day he died. He was referring to "close quarter" fighting techniques British instructors taught Canadian soldiers as they trained prior to the invasion of Italy.

As I understand it, his sentiment is shared by many of those who fought in the Battle of Ortona. "The damn Limeys (Bert always referred to the British as Limeys as did many of his peers) told us that when tanks or artillery can't make it down the narrow streets of some of the ancient Italian towns those of us in the infantry should stick close to the buildings and make our way down the streets clearing out the enemy as we go."

Here he usually paused before shaking his head and saying, "We lost a hell of a lot of good men following those instructions."

Bert survived Ortona and the rest of the Italian campaign, but he was one of the fortunate ones. Tragically, 1,375 Canadians died and 964 were wounded in the Battle of Ortona and the surrounding area often described as the Italian Stalingrad. Total Canadian casualties in the Ortona and nearby Moro River area during December 1943 were nearly 5,000. They called it "Bloody December".

The reason for the fierce fighting were orders from Hitler that the 1st German Parachute Division defending Ortona must stand fast and not retreat.

The house to house fighting is vicious and the Canadian death toll would be much higher if the men didn't quickly scrap their instructions about "close quarter fighting" and invent what they call "mouse-holing". Instead of exposing themselves to sniper fire on the streets, the Canadians figure out that since many Ortona houses share walls, they can blast holes through those walls, usually in the top floors, and proceed from house to house without risking the streets.

On December 24, members of the Seaforth Highlands Division are summoned, one by one, from the battle for a Christmas Eve dinner in a partially destroyed church. Sadly some are killed on their way to that church, but several hundred men did make it there safely and paused for a few moments for a meal of roast pork and Christmas pudding as Will Gildersleeve plays Silent ght on the church organ.

ree days later the Germans flee. The Canadians have won again, but at terrible cost.

Fifty-five years later some of the Canadian vets who were at that Christmas celebration in 1943 take the trip back to Ortona to share another Christmas Eve dinner, this time with some of the German soldiers against whom they fought. Many hands are shaken, many backs are patted, many stories are told, and many tears are shed!

Not only did listeners to my show on CFRA Radio and readers of my good friend the late Earl McRae's column in the Ottawa Sun donate all the money to send those vets back to the 1998 Christmas Eve Dinner, enough money was donated ($180,000) to design, build, ship and install a very moving monument to all those Canadian troops who took part in what was one of the deadliest battles of the Second World War.

That monument can be seen today in the main town square in the heart of a totally reconstructed Ortona. A gift from ordinary people to extraordinary men!

CANADA 150

THE RED RIVER CART

The American covered wagon may receive most of the publicity. It's featured in most of the western movies and stories, but it is no match for Canada's Red River cart when it comes to durability, versatility, ingenuity of design and manufacture, and noise!

The Red River cart is actually a fantastic bit of pioneer architecture. It looks like a huge basket set between two large wheels, pulled by an ox or Indian pony.

Nothing can top it for sheer ingenuity, since not one fragment of metal is used. Every last bit of the Red River cart is constructed from local hardwoods and buffalo hides. The hides are soaked in water for many days, beaten until soft, then fastened to the hardwood rims of the carts and left to dry. When the hides harden they are almost as tough and durable as iron.

Another feature of the Red River cart is that if you remove the wheels it makes a pretty good raft.

There is another thing about the carts. You are never in danger of being run over by one, unless you are stone deaf.

Without metal there are no bearings. When the wheels turn, it is wood rubbing on wood, with perhaps a bit of bear grease stuffed in along with the prairie dust and gumbo. The noise, it is said, was sufficient to deter a band of attacking Indians.

When they began to organize them into trains of as many as four to five hundred, strung out across the prairie, you could hear them coming for well over a hundred miles.

But the little carts served our pioneer forefathers well. They played a vital role in the settlement of the Canadian West and appropriately enough, the first manufacturing plant in the Canadian West was a Red River cart factory at Whitehorse Plains, some ten miles west of Fort Garry.

A VERY CLOSE CALL!

There's perhaps no better illustration of how careful we must be when selling our natural resources than what almost happened at Niagara Falls.

As we enter the 20th century, electrical power is pretty much a novelty. An American company launches a small electrical generating station at Niagara Falls in 1882 but quickly goes bankrupt. Ten years later, a Canadian company begins using power from Niagara Falls to operate trains running between Queenston and Chippewa but for the most part the water thundering over the Falls is ignored.

So when an American firm offers a few thousand dollars to Ontario for the rights to all electrical power produced by Niagara Falls many politicians rub their hands in delight and despite objections from a few, we come within days of giving up all rights forever to what was to become one of the world's major sources of electrical power.

Thank heavens Thomas (Carbide) Willson steps into the debate with some common sense.

Willson is a famous Canadian inventor, the man who discovered how to make acetylene gas, built and operated Canada's first hydroelectric plant, the largest in North America at Merriton, Ontario a suburb of St. Catharines.

Keenly aware of the potential of electrical power, he fights bitterly against those who would sell all our rights to Niagara Falls. There are many who consider him outrageous for turning down what seems a large sum of money, but Willson sticks to his guns, recruits politicians to his side, lobbies in the press and elsewhere and finally wins.

Canada retains rights to hydroelectric power produced by Niagara Falls and Willson goes on to pioneer the production of electrical power throughout North America.

Largely forgotten today, Willson is one of the world's greatest inventors and innovators. He owned the first car ever seen on Ottawa streets and patented more than 70 different inventions. A house he built at Meech Lake just north of Ottawa, was converted into the Government Convention Centre in which the famous (or infamous) Meech Lake Accord was struck.

Those ruins you see today at Meech Lake are the remnants of a superphosphate generating plant and an acid condensation tower he built.

But his greatest legacy surely are the millions of kilowatts of electrical power from Niagara Falls that keep the lights burning across much of Ontario and even into the United States where they still rue the fact they don't own it all!

THE SEVEN MILE RIDE

No account of Canada's early days would be complete without a story of the famous "Rivermen".

At a time when logging is about the only employment available, armies of men cut giant pines in winter, roll them to the edge of rivers and lakes, and then in spring ride the logs, herding giant timber-rafts to sawmills along the Ottawa River and even as far as Quebec City!

It is the ambition of almost every boy growing up in Eastern Ontario's Glengarry County to become a Riverman. Riding logs down raging rivers is about the most exciting thing they can imagine. From a very early age they practice on some of the smaller rivers in the area, taking many a dip in cold waters as their skills improve.

Norman MacRae and his brothers are bigger and stronger than most. Norman in particular, develops the ability to balance on a log then flip it over completely, end for end.

His abilities undoubtedly save his life when the MacRae brothers are contracted to "herd" a two mile long timber raft from Georgian Bay to Ottawa through unfamiliar waters.

Norman, his heavy trousers tucked into high corked boots, his head topped by a knitted cap with a tassel, rides his log without fear. On either side are small boats, called pointers, each manned by eight strong rowers. From time to time, Norman and Andrew wave at each other as they ride their logs down the fast moving river. The rowers are singing the famous Glengarry Boat Song.

Suddenly the stream widens out. The current picks up. Norman begins shooting far ahead of the boats, then around a bend—a great expanse of churning open water. A log tossed by the current slams into his; only his tremendous strength and skill prevent him being tossed into the frigid water. The cold wind, whipping off ice covered Georgian Bay, chills him to the bone. His hands become numb.

All his life, Norman has felt directed in a crisis by a voice he calls the "Spirit". Now it seems to be his mother's voice calling him, "Hang on Norman, hang on man!" And hang on he does as the waves crash over him spinning the log every which way, up waves and down.

Norman MacRae, pike pole in hand for balance, rides that log for more than seven miles. One misjudged spin, one small mistake would be the end of him.

When his brother finds him, Norman is lying face down on his log, unconscious, his arms trailing in the calm waters of a bay.

Later Norman explains it was the spirit that saved him—"I heard the spirit Andy, the spirit spoke to me. I heard Mother say, hang on Normie lad, hang on."

It is a bedtime story that Glengarry mothers still tell their little children.

CANADA 150

THE CLOSE SHAVE

The "Silver Fox" Dick Irvin, coach of the Montreal Canadiens, is in a great mood. Not only has his team defeated the Chicago Black Hawks, but he's been able to track down the Chicago breeder of championship Golden Hamburg chickens and persuade him to sell a dozen chicks.

Irvin's only problem now as he boards a train to head home, is how to get those little fluffy chicks across the border into Canada without having to fill out a fist full of papers. He phones fellow chicken fancier Canadiens General Manager Frank Selke back in Montreal and is told, "Just pack the chicks in a small cardboard box and carry it with you. If they ask, tell them at the border you've just got a few sandwiches for the boys. Make sure you've got a saucer or something," says Selke, "so when you get into Canada you can take them into the washroom and give them a drink a couple times. They'll be fine till you reach Montreal."

They forget one thing. The chicks, apparently quite content in their nice, warm little home begin loudly peeping in appreciation, or maybe concern, who knows, but it's apparent the peeping will be a dead giveaway that there's something other than sandwiches in that little box when border officials start checking for ID.

Roused from slumber, a couple of the players become intrigued and offer advice. One of them suggests the chicks must be peeping for their mother, but his clucking noise does nothing but earn a few guffaws. Nothing they do quells the peeping and the conductor is seen moving in their direction.

Certain he is about to lose his champion chicks and probably get raked over the coals for trying to sneak live animals over the border, in desperation, Irvin throws his jacket over the box but that only seems to ramp up the volume a bit more.

By this time most of the players know what's going on and begin chuckling and poking each other in delighted anticipation of "Coach" being the one on the receiving end of a solid verbal body check or two!

Just then, the ever dapper Elmer Lach comes strolling out of the washroom, still running his brand new electric shaver over his face. Unaware of the unfolding drama, Elmer leans over and starts to ask what that peeping noise is when suddenly there is a hush from beneath the coat. A little puzzled by it all, Elmer straightens and begins strolling back to his seat. As he leaves, the peeping starts up again.

The light goes on in Irvin's head. "Quick", he says, "give me that razor!" Elmer shrugs his shoulders and hands it over.

A few minutes later as the conductor collects and punches his ticket, Dick Irvin is busily shaving away non-existent stubble with Elmer Lach's nice new razor whose buzzing seems to have entranced the chicks into total silence.

Unfortunately by the time they reach Montreal, Irvin's face is raw from six more forced shaving episodes each time a conductor walks through the coach.

The face is fine however about a year later when one of those chicks wins the "Best of Breed" award at the prestigious Royal Winter Fair in Toronto. As luck would have it, it's the bird Irvin named Buzz!

THE LAST SPIKE

Buried in a drawer someplace in our house lies a gold painted railway spike, acquired at considerable cost from the souvenir shop in the middle of the Rocky Mountains at Craigellachie, BC.

It is, of course, not the most famous railway spike in the world, driven into a railway tie on November 7, 1885 by Donald Smith (later Lord Strathcona), thus connecting the eastern and western sections of the Canadian Pacific Railway.

The picture of the top-hatted, white-bearded Smith, sledge hammer in hand pounding away at that last spike is featured in almost every Canadian history book ever written. Stories have been written, movies made about the "Craigellachie Kid" (Edward Mallandaine), the hatted boy poking his head out from the crowd of hatted and mostly bearded spectators at this historic event.

But the spike itself? What happened to it?

Even noted author and historian the late Pierre Berton in his bestselling book, "The Last Spike", wasn't able to track down the legendary spike, despite considerable research. In fairness, however, new information indicates Berton may have come close to finding it.

But the mystery may be over.

The Globe and Mail newspaper claims to have found it saying:

"As it turns out, the Globe has learned what is believed to be the legendary last spike resides in a safety deposit box in a Winnipeg

bank. Fashioned into the handle of a carving knife and silver plated to enhance its ceremonial appearance, the spike has been in the family of Canadian patent officer W.J. Lynch for three generations".

According to the Globe story the spike was yanked from the ground immediately after the photographs were taken and given to Edward Beatty, the first Canadian born president of the CPR. It was apparently stolen from Beatty's desk and after several different owners, finally ended up in the possession of the former clerk of the Legislative Assembly of the Yukon, W.J. Lynch.

The Globe story first appeared in 2012. Whether Mr. Lynch still has it is not clear.

Actually the last spike is the second one that Smith whacked away at. The remains of the first one that he partially missed and bent is now on display at the Canada Science and Technology Museum in Ottawa.

And as for Edward Mallandaine, a.k.a. the "Craigellachie Kid", he was 18 when that famous picture was taken, half frozen from an overnight boxcar ride, determined to take part in history.

Four years later he stakes out a 180 acre farm overlooking Kootenay Lake, helps establish the town of Creston, marries the town's first teacher, lives a happy life and dies in 1949 at the age of 82.

The railway, of course is still there, still serving our Country very well.

THE POEM

In Flanders fields the poppies blow
Between the crosses, row on row,
That mark our place; and in the sky
The larks still bravely singing fly
Scarce heard amid the guns below.

We are the dead: Short days ago,
We lived, felt dawn, saw sunset glow,
Loved and were loved: and now we lie
In Flanders fields!

Take up our quarrel with the foe
To you, from failing hands, we throw
The torch: be yours to hold it high
If ye break faith with us who die,
We shall not sleep, though poppies grow
In Flanders fields.

Composed by Colonel John McCrae on the battlefront,
May 3, 1915 during the second battle of Ypres, Belgium.

Is there a more loved poem in the world? It's doubtful.

First pencilled on a torn out page of a dispatch book it was written in sorrow just a day after Colonel McCrae's close friend Alexis Helmer was killed.

The night before at the gravesite, in the absence of a chaplain, McCrae recited from memory a few passages from the Church of England's Order of the Burial of the Dead:

"I am the resurrection and the life, saith the Lord; he that believeth in me, though he were dead, yet shall he live; and whosoever liveth and believeth in me shall never die".

The British publication Punch, recognizing its beauty, printed In Flanders Fields in heavy-leaded type used only on great occasions. Within a few weeks the poem had spread throughout the English speaking world.

McCrae's commanding officer Major General E.W.B. Morrison wrote, "This poem was literally born of fire and blood during the hottest phase of the Second Battle of Ypres. My headquarters was in a trench on the top of the bank of the Ypres Canal and John had his dressing station in a hole dug in the foot of the bank. During periods in the battle, wounded men actually rolled down the bank into his dressing station. Many times during the 16 days of battle he and I watched the chaplains burying their dead whenever there was a lull."

General Morrison says they often did hear the larks singing high in the sky between the crashing of the shells.

The wooden crosses have now been replaced by marble ones and a memorial chapel has been built near the spot where McCrae wrote his famous lines.

McCrae was gassed during the fighting in Ypres and just three years later died of pneumonia and meningitis.

The idea of wearing red poppies to mark Remembrance Day sprang from his famous poem.

CANADA 150

MILITARY THUMBS DOWN
FOR AIRPLANES

"Aeroplanes are just a fad. They have absolutely no role to play in the Canadian military. The Canadian Government will not support in any way any kind of aviation industry."

That pretty well sums up Canada's response to a plea by Alexander Graham Bell that aeroplanes could have a major military role in any future war and because of that the Government should become involved in the science and development of flight.

On March 27, 1909 Bell addresses the Canadian Club of Ottawa and gives one of the most prophetic speeches in the history of this Country.

In attendance is the cream of Canada's political and military elite including Prime Minister Sir Wilfred Laurier, Robert Borden, leader of the Official Opposition, most cabinet ministers and such notables as Sir Sandford Fleming.

Listen to what Bell says, keeping in mind that the First World War is nearly six years away:

"Dirigible balloons have features that should make us pause. It is a thought, it seems to me, for the British nation, supreme upon the waters, to consider that a balloon, such as that of Count Zeppelin, could float over London, and all the British fleet could not prevent it. Of course, we do not know what Great Britain is doing. But the success of such a machine as that, means more to Great Britain than to any other major power, because when these machines are used for purposes of war, sea power becomes secondary to air power. The nation that controls the air will ultimately be the foremost nation of the world. So, the success of the dirigible balloon, even though to my belief it is on a wrong basis, being lighter than air, is of the greatest importance to mankind."

His speech, which by the way, also confirmed that the telephone had indeed been invented in Canada, was loudly applauded; and Bell, rather reluctantly, is invited to arrange a demonstration of the Silver Dart's abilities during that summer at the Camp Petawawa military base.

On the morning of August 2, 1909, the Silver Dart is paraded in front of a large group of top military and Government officials then makes five flights over the base. She flies about 50 miles an hour at an altitude of 50 feet demonstrating her ability to turn and flies distances each time of about a mile.

Four of the flights are perfect but the fifth is a disaster. The Silver Dart's wheels become caught in some loose sand upon landing and she flips up onto her nose and is wrecked beyond repair. J.A.D. McCurdy, who pilots all five flights, suffers a broken nose, the only injury of his long career in the air.

The accident gives the assembled military officers the out they are looking for. Even though four of the flights have been perfect, it's ruled that the fifth flight was the official one and since it had been a failure, the test failed and therefore it's decided that there is no role in the military for airplanes.

Thus ends the life of the Silver Dart, sacrificed in the name of King and Country. Today a monument marks the spot of her death and proclaims it to be the birthplace of Canadian military aviation.

The plaque is obviously wrong. Not only was it not the birth of Canadian military aviation, quite the opposite, but it claims that Casey Baldwin flew the Silver Dart along with McCurdy. In fact it was only McCurdy at the controls.

It takes several more years before the Canadian military finally wakes up and decides there might be a role for military aviation after all and in a strange twist of fate, not only does Canada provide many of the war "aces" in both World Wars, it becomes the home for much of the pilot training and during the Second World War supplies thousands of fighter aircraft.

Alexander Graham Bell died in 1922 but lived long enough to see his grim predictions realized during the First World War where military aviation played an increasingly vital role.

A fly-past by R.C.A.F. Sabre Jets in 1961 paid tribute to the Honorable J.A.D. McCurdy as his ashes were laid to rest not far from where, so many years ago at Baddeck, the Silver Dart first lurched into the air!

THE NEWFOUNDLAND
FLORENCE NIGHTINGALE

"To a future generation there will be few aspects of our present way of life quite as mystifying as our reasons for heaping fame on a woman. And surely, if our grandchildren have the intelligence to survive the chaos we will have left them, they will be particularly caustic of our custom of lavishing wealth and worship on one of the opposite sex because of a pretty face or a super bosom or a voice with some kind of squeak or quiver in it. Nor will they be able to understand why we have given so little recognition to many of our truly magnificent women; those whose courage and sacrifice and inspiration have made this world, or some part of it, a better place to live.

And in that more sensible day it is entirely possible that Newfoundland's Nurse Bennett will have become the kind of heroine which the school books love to make into legend.

Myra Bennett, in her 50 years on the Northwest Coast, faced so many emergencies she didn't have the time to record them all. In most of those emergencies she was desperately alone. And death itself was often the challenger!"

From the book "Don't have your baby in the Dory! A biography of Myra Bennett" by H. Gordon Green.

In fact, more than one of the more than 5,000 babies that Nurse Bennett delivered in her more than 50 years on the windswept lonely Newfoundland coast was born in a dory, as time ran out in a desperate dash for a far off hospital bed. Many of those 5,000 drew their first breaths on the Bennett kitchen table in the tiny outport of Daniel's Harbour; a table where many an angry boil was lanced, many a wound stitched up and sadly the table where some drew their last breath.

Nurse Bennett, who became known as the Newfoundland Florence Nightingale, was the only medical help along the desolate, northwest coast of Newfoundland for 200 miles.

For more than 50 years she delivered babies, set broken limbs, treated infections and afflictions of all kinds, by her own estimation pulled between 3,000 and 4,000 teeth, taught hygiene and was available at any hour of the day or night for medical emergencies of all kinds. Myra herself once wrote, "The need for medical help is beyond my description".

Some of those emergencies required dangerous and extremely uncomfortable trips to distant villages or ports. Sometimes in these isolated communities Nurse Bennett was confronted with a major problem for which she had no training—a kind of witchcraft. They called it "charming": A green ribbon around your neck was believed by some, to cure a serious nosebleed. A willow twig wrapped around a wrist would "charm" away the flu. Myra quickly learned how to deal with "charming". She simply suggested that since the problem could be "charmed" away she might as well leave and began to pack up her equipment. This usually persuaded the afflicted to give traditional medicine a try!

Myra arrived in Daniel's Harbour from England in May, 1921; her first winter was one of the coldest on record in Newfoundland, which she refers to in her diary entry recorded in mid-January, 1922. The following is taken directly from that diary which recounts what was a typical couple of days.

"Called to Parson's Pond. It was a dreadful day and I suffered greatly with cold although warmly wrapped up and drawn by horse. Reached destination at about six p.m. and saw several patients. Retired at twelve thirty midnight, very fatigued.

Left at seven thirty a.m. to return home. Hibbert Caines took me to Portland Creek and Alec came there for me. (Alec was Angus' brother. Angus had gone away hunting on Tuesday). I was desperately tired but did some teeth extractions on the return journey.

Was called to Bellburns. Was drawn half way by Nell Biggen but had to walk the rest which I found was as much as I could manage.

Extracted twelve teeth for Mrs. Alice House. Spent the rest of the day blouse making and resting.

Extracted one tooth for Gertrude House.

Mrs. Grant House began to be sick at four a.m. and I got up. She was safely delivered of a boy at one p.m. Steamer called at Daniel's Harbour at three p.m. but sea was too rough to land any freight. I had a very small mail.

Rather a stormy day. Steamer passed us without calling on her return trip to Bay of Islands. Jim Bennett hit his foot with an axe and made a deep cut through the instep necessitating three stitches.

Nora Biggen came with a septic index finger which I opened and drained."

The Angus referred to in Myra's diary was her husband who built them a little house in Daniel's Harbour, a house soon filled with patients, some of whom stayed recuperating for days or even weeks. There were times when both Myra and Angus had to sleep on the kitchen floor, all beds occupied by the sick.

One man was dropped off by fellow workers who was so ill with a kidney infection Myra was certain he would die. He left the Bennet house six weeks later, completely recovered.

Overcoming accepted custom was another major battle for Myra. When she arrived she was shocked to see newborn babies immediately turned over for breast feeding to another woman. It was believed that for the first three days of a child's life it was preferable to have it suckle at the breast of what they called a "nursing mother". It took a long time for Myra to convince them that a newborn needed its mother's milk, especially in those first few days. She insisted that "The first milk is different and it is what God means the new baby to have. If the child doesn't get that special first milk he is going to suffer and maybe even die."

The message finally took effect and infant mortality rates in Myra's area dropped dramatically.

Myra's is an incredible story of sacrifice and dedication. Even after her retirement in 1953 she continued to provide medical assistance to anyone who required it. She raised three children, launched a child's choir, won many awards including the Order of Canada, was presented with the King George V1 Medal by the King himself, and died in 1990 at the age of 100.

Today, the house that Angus built and was often jammed from top to bottom with patients has become the Nurse Myra Bennett Heritage House Museum.

When I suggested Nurse Bennett as a candidate to become the first woman (other than the Queen) to appear on Canadian currency I was told she was ineligible because most of her service occurred when Newfoundland was not a part of Canada. I'd be interested to know what you think!

THE LOWLIEST PROFESSION

There was a time in this Country when school teaching was considered the lowliest of all the professions. In fact it was not even considered a profession but something you had to do if you couldn't find a "real" job!

Here's a description of early pioneer schools and teachers contained in an 1899 edition of the Prince Edward Island Magazine. (Yearly subscription 50 cents).

"Usually persons of shipwrecked character and blasted prospects in life, after every other resource failed, became a teacher. Sometimes a man, too proud to beg, too upright to steal, would consent to wield the birch.

If the population of a village moved away, the schoolhouse moved with it. In those days teachers would compete for schools, not schools for teachers though the lot of a teacher was not a very happy or profitable one. He was boarded from house-to-house and was held in no respect whatsoever but rather as a handyman.

One teacher who had been a court crier is said to have summoned his children to school with "Oyez-Oyez-Oyez, come into the school." That particular teacher dismissed school at noon and again in the afternoon with grace.

One district has a schoolhouse that had been a cabin on a wrecked ship, the teacher had been shipwrecked as well. His pride was in having the loudest school on the Island and insisted that his children recite everything in unison at the top of their voices.

In these schools the birch rod and fool's cap were the chief methods of discipline. Fighting boys were made to "paly-wrap-jacket". This expression means that each was armed with a switch and made to beat each other until one was exhausted.

In some country posts, the teacher was a farmer who got up early to do his chores then went to school for a rest."

Pretty obvious that despite all stories to the contrary, the good old days did have a few drawbacks!

THE PATRIOT AND THE FLQ

The FLQ murderers have befouled the name of one of Canada's bravest patriots.

Here in Canada, several attempts were made to copy the Americans and throw off the British yoke. The rebellions of Upper and Lower Canada (Ontario and Quebec) were all destined to fail. The attempts in Ontario by William Lyon Mackenzie are well known but few people in English Canada are aware that there was also a rebellion in Quebec that ended in terrible bloodshed. They certainly aren't aware that the men and women who kidnapped Paul Cross and brutally murdered Pierre Laporte during the FLQ crisis named their group and slandered the name of one of the bravest patriots in Canada's history.

Jean Olivier Chenier is a country doctor from St. Eustache, about 20 miles north of Montreal, who fervently believes that Canada should abolish British rule and follow the example of the Americans and declare independence.

He joins such well known French Canadian leaders as Morin, Viger, Lafontaine and Papineau in planning a Lower Canada (Quebec) rebellion to coincide with the one to be launched by Mackenzie in Toronto. Together they believe they can overthrow the British and form a republic.

But Chenier is betrayed by his own leadership. He is left alone to lead the revolt while all the more famous men wait safely in the United States.

Undaunted, Chenier leads a force of about 300 men to fight the British at St. Eustache, but without the promised help from those who have deserted him, they are doomed.

The Red Coats set fire to Chenier's church headquarters. Refusing to surrender, the patriots led by Chenier, rush from the flames and make a last desperate stand in the church graveyard, often firing from behind tombstones.

There is no quarter given. No prisoners taken. The patriots, to the last man, are killed. The rebellion is over.

Chenier has almost been forgotten, while streets, parks and buildings bear the names of those who turned tail and hid in his hour of need. A small neglected statue in Old Montreal is all that stands today to recall his memory.

Until a cell of the FLQ dredged up his name during the kidnap and murder of Pierre Laporte. The murderers called themselves the Chenier Cell.

Jean Olivier Chenier deserves far better!

GOODBYE COLONEL BY

Even as Colonel John By enters the Smiths Falls Locks on his triumphant, historic inaugural cruise along the Rideau Canal he built, back home in London they're signing the papers to fire him in disgrace.

By, of course, doesn't know what fate has in store for him, neither does the large crowd that has gathered at the Smiths Falls lock as the steamship paddlewheeler Pumper is flawlessly locked through, with Colonel By standing proudly on the bow. With By to help him celebrate his incredible feat are his wife Esther and his two daughters, 13 year old Esther and 11 year old Harriet.

It's early morning, May 25, 1832 when an 18 pound cannon is fired from a promontory overlooking Smiths Falls to mark the official opening of the canal linking Kingston with Ottawa. The Pumper fires its small cannon in proud response.

By turns to his wife and says he cannot believe that it was only four years ago when he last passed through Smiths Falls, on that occasion in a birch bark canoe as he mapped out the route the Canal would take.

Even by today's standards with satellites and modern, powerful dredges and other equipment it is an engineering marvel. UNESCO World Heritage describes the Rideau Canal as "Creative Genius".

Two hundred and two kilometres (123 miles) long with 47 locks the Rideau Canal today is the oldest continuously used canal in North America.

As just one example of the magnitude of his feat, the huge dam at Jones Falls (360 feet long, 60 feet high) was the largest one of its kind in the British Empire, perhaps the world at the time, but none of this is sufficient to save him from the disaster which awaits him back home in London.

Incredibly, it is May 25, 1832, the same day that By so proudly sails through the Smiths Falls Locks, that the British Treasury advises the Government that:

"The Lords of the Treasury desire that the Master General and Board will take immediate steps for removing Colonel By from any further superintendence over any part of the works for making Canal Communications in Canada. My Lords further desire that Colonel By may be forthwith ordered to return to this country that he may be called upon to afford such explanations as My Lords may consider necessary upon this important subject."

The subject referred to was the claim that By had spent far more money building the Canal than was budgeted.

The fact that the budget imposed by the British treasury was entirely unrealistic and that the main complaint against By was lodged by a disgruntled alcoholic former employee fired by By wasn't even considered when the decision was made to relieve him of his duties.

It wasn't until August that By received the summons to return home. He is thrilled, believing that he is going to return to London a hero. When he is finally able to return in November he fully expects a major promotion and quite possibly be granted a knighthood.

Instead, his career is over the moment he set foot on English soil. Despite the fact that various parliamentary committees exonerated him and ruled that he had done his job properly his reputation is ruined, he receives no promotion, no honours and in deep frustration and anger he retires to his estate in Sussex.

CANADA 150

He dies only three years later a terribly wronged and deeply disappointed man at the age of 53.

His greatest honour is the memorial erected by his wife in St. Alban's Church

Which reads:

> *Sacred to the memory of*
>
> *Lieutenant Colonel John By, Royal Engineers*
>
> *Of Shernfold Park in this parish.*
>
> *Zealous and distinguished in his profession,*
>
> *Tender and affectionate as a husband and father,*
>
> *And lamented by the poor, he resigned his soul to his Maker,*
>
> *In full reliance on the merits of his blessed Redeemer,*
>
> *On 1st, February, 1836, aged 53 years,*
>
> *After a long and painful illness,*
>
> *Brought on by his indefatigable zeal and devotion in the service*
>
> *Of his King and Country, in Upper Canada*

CANADA 150

THE PHONE SONG

Lady Dufferin, wife of Canada's third Governor General since Confederation is a very popular woman, probably the most loved and respected occupant of Rideau Hall in our history, so when Lady Dufferin wants something, chances are very good Lady Dufferin will get it.

Which is why telephone history is made at Rideau Hall.

It's about a year since Alexander Graham Bell made that first historic long distance phone call between Brantford and Paris, Ontario. Most people still think the whole idea of being able to talk to someone at the end of a wire is pretty silly, nothing but a fad.

But Lady Dufferin as a modern woman and social leader, decides she should find out what all the buzz is about. "I'd like to try one of these new phone things," she says, or words to that effect. So a temporary line is hooked up between Rideau Hall and an office in the Public Works Department a few blocks away.

As luck would have it, the G.G's wife is treated to the singing voice of a young clerk, quite possibly the first such musical transmission in history. Lady Dufferin, who is a bit of a song writer herself when not hosting grand soirees, is so delighted at the beautiful voice, she orders that the temporary phone line be replaced with a permanent one. History is made again. It becomes the first permanent private telephone line in Ottawa and one of the first in Canada.

Prime Minister Alexander Mackenzie is not pleased to see the bill for this cross his desk. He's had a phone in his office for a couple months and never used it.

History doesn't record how long that first phone line lasted, we suspect until Lord and Lady Dufferin left Ottawa for Russia in 1878.

A bit more telephone history is made in Ottawa, when during the Ottawa Exhibition in the fall of 1877 thousands flock into a building in Lansdowne Park to hear the first public demonstration of a long distance phone call. A phone is installed at one end of a large building with a line strung across the rafters to a phone at the other end.

Newspaper reports of the day tell us that the large "throng assembled in the Hall were galvanized at the ability of transporting the human voice along a thin metal wire."

By the way, the first Federal Government switchboard was installed four years later with 50 lines to various offices.

LAURA SECORD AND THE INDIANS

Laura Secord gets all the credit, but in fact it was a group of native Indians who helped and guided her on her famous jaunt through the bush and swamps.

It isn't widely known that Laura wasn't any spring chicken when she herded her cow through enemy lines to warn of an impending attack. In fact, history records her as 38 and the mother of five.

The year is 1813, Canada and the U.S. have been at war for nearly a year; things aren't going very well for Canadians. The Americans have occupied the village of Queenston where some are billeted in the home of Mrs. James Secord, a local seamstress.

Mrs. Secord overhears officers planning to attack the Canadian forces stationed at Beaver Dams about 20 miles away. Her husband, being wounded in an earlier battle, is unable to walk so the next morning, with almost unbelievable ingenuity and courage, she releases a cow from the barn and drives it ahead of her as she sets out for a 20 mile walk through thick bush and mosquito infested swamps to warn the troops at Beaver Dams.

She is accosted by sentries but is allowed to continue, claiming she is just returning a lost cow. Dressed only in her petticoat, a yellow kimono and flimsy slippers, she appears to be anything but a spy or courier.

She plods on through the hot June day, sometimes having to forge swollen streams. Finding a bridge washed out, she creeps across on a log.

As night falls, she blunders into an Indian encampment. With a tomahawk poised above her head she persuades the warriors that their only hope of safety depends upon Canada winning the war and preserving Indian Territory. This doesn't take much persuading since the Indians are only too well aware that the Americans are wiping out native populations in the United States and will likely do the same in Canada if victorious.

The Indians provide her with better footwear then guide her to the headquarters of Colonel James Fitzgibbons (near present day Brock University) in time to warn them of an impending attack.

The next day, the invading Americans are ambushed by the Indians who are quickly joined by Fitzgibbons and his men. A number of Americans are killed and about 500 taken prisoner. It is a major defeat for the Americans and hastens the end of the war.

FROM CHORUS GIRL TO HERO

Mona Parsons was betrayed twice. First by a Nazi sympathizer and then by her husband! Thank goodness they are finally building a statue in her honour. What an incredible story it is!

Born in Nova Scotia, Mona studied acting then moved to New York City where she danced as a Ziegfeld chorus girl in the famous Ziegfeld Follies. She later became a nurse and married Dutch millionaire Willem Leonhardt and moved with him to Laren, Holland in 1937.

In May, 1940 Mona joins the Dutch resistance movement, dismisses her servants and converts the top floor of her home into a hiding place for downed Allied airmen. A tiny room behind the closet in the master bedroom is turned into a temporary emergency shelter if the Nazis came looking. From there the pilots are smuggled during the night to Leiden, where fishing boats take them to rendezvous with British submarines.

Tragically, a Nazi sympathizer exposes the entire operation, two American airmen, after six days at Mona's home, are captured by the Gestapo and Mona is arrested, charged with treason and sentenced to death by firing squad. The sentence is commuted to life in prison with hard labour.

On March 6, 1942 Mona and several other prisoners are transported to Anrath Prison in Germany, then transferred to Wiedenbruck where she works on an assembly line creating plywood wings for small craft. She becomes ill several times and undergoes terrible hardship and starvation.

On February 6, 1945 the prisoners at Wiedenbruck are herded onto a train bound for another prison in Vechta. Here she writes:

"The first year I was ill a lot, weighed only about 94 pounds and was green – night sweats, coughing and diarrhoea every day for 3 ½ months and often vomiting. Tears have run down my cheeks from hunger. When the diarrhoea got better I was given a pint of soup extra – made from turnip and potato peelings – every day for six months and my vitamin tablets which I had been allowed to keep with me. There were no medicines to be had. We slept four in a tiny cell built for one. In all the years of imprisonment I slept always on a straw sack on the floor.

I was in solitary once for two weeks, for writing a letter in English. Fortunately no one could read English, otherwise another prisoner might have been involved. I got out of it by saying it was only a little story I was writing to amuse myself. We were not allowed to have pencil or paper. Practically four years of isolation. During my first contact with people – after throwing off my half-witted act – I felt only half conscious of all that went on about me. My body was shaky – my brain seemed quite numb – thoroughly incapable of absorbing what was said to me. My head spun. It just seemed too much, all of a sudden. We'd had literally no brain stimulation all these years – we were forbidden to talk during our twelve hour working day – at night too tired to do anything but crawl into bed. Even when we weren't too tired to talk – we'd have little to talk about. We heard no news scarcely. We were not even allowed to have books."

On March 24, 1945, as Allied forces bomb the prison camp, Mona escapes with young Dutch Baroness Wendelien van Boetzelaer. What follows is an incredible feat. Although she speaks fluent German, Mona is afraid to reveal her Canadian accent, so she pretends to be the young woman's mute aunt. Since the roads are often jammed with refugees escaping bombed out towns, they are able to walk about 125 miles to the Dutch border, often sleeping in barns and relying for food on refugee camps that are set up to assist those fleeing the carnage behind them. They would likely have been shot on the spot if caught.

The two escapees part at the Dutch border. Mona is able to track down a resistance fighter who leads her to the North Nova Scotia Highlanders who are liberating Holland. She is half dead from exhaustion, hypothermia and malnutrition, but she is alive and she dances with joy!

During the war it was a Nazi sympathizer who betrayed her. When the war ends the betrayal is at the hands of her husband. After his death in 1956, Mona learns that he had left one quarter of his estate to a mistress. A son he had with the other woman, under Dutch law, is entitled to three quarters of Leonhardt's multi-million dollar estate. Mona is left with nothing and can do nothing about it.

Air Chief Marshal Lord Arthur Tedder of the R.C.A.F. on behalf of the British people and General Dwight Eisenhower on behalf of the United States both pay tribute to Mona and thank her for saving Allied lives, but she is forced to live in poverty until returning to Nova Scotia in 1957 where she marries Major General Harry Foster and moves to the lovely little town of Chester not far from Halifax.

In May of 2017, a statue to Mona Parsons was scheduled to be erected in Wolfville, Nova Scotia not far from where she was buried in November of 1976. It pays tribute to Mona's courage and sacrifice and notes that she is the only Canadian civilian woman ever to spend time in a German Prisoner of War camp!

Sculptor Nistal Prem de Boer decided to capture that moment when she first met those Nova Scotia soldiers and knew she was finally safe. The statue depicts her kicking off the clogs they have given her for her badly damaged feet and even though weakened and very emaciated, dancing with joy!

BATTLE OF THE ST. LAWRENCE

Even today there is great reluctance by governments of all stripes to admit that not only did German submarines do battle in the St. Lawrence River during WWII but they managed to sink 23 vessels there with a great loss of life.

This reluctance may be because, above all else, it reveals how badly prepared we were to defend our inland waters at the outbreak of the War and how much we depended upon the United States to do the defending for us, something that is still very much a fact of life!

The first casualty of the Battle of the St. Lawrence was on May 12, 1942 when the British freighter Nicoya was torpedoed at the mouth of the St. Lawrence several kilometres off Anticosti Island. The Dutch freighter Leto was sunk in the same vicinity several hours later.

As evidence of how poorly equipped we were is the fact that before those sinkings, the Gulf of St. Lawrence was guarded by only four RCN (Royal Canadian Navy) warships, a minesweeper, two small motor launches and an armed yacht.

Four corvettes were added to the defences but it wasn't nearly enough to patrol the vast expanse of the Gulf and the River itself.

There were demands in Parliament that the RCN provide more protection for our territorial waters, but the main responsibility of our Navy was to escort the convoys of ships carrying desperately needed supplies and food to Britain.

The carnage continued. In July 1942 one submarine sank three ships within half an hour in the Gulf. In late August two U-boats made a raid on the St. Lawrence River sinking nine ships and damaging another in a two week period.

Residents along the Gaspe coast and further inland were often startled as ships battled just off their shores. Ships were on fire, heavy explosions shook windows. Bodies and debris washed up on shore.

Censors denied media reporting the incidents. The only news came from local gossip. Blackouts along the coast were strictly enforced. The St. Lawrence Valley was very clearly at war but most Canadians were not allowed to know it.

In October of 1942 the Newfoundland Railway passenger ferry SS Caribou was torpedoed and sunk in the Cabot Strait with a heavy loss of life.

It wasn't just a naval battle. In November, 1942 the Germans managed to land a spy at New Carlisle, Quebec. Werner von Janowski was captured at the railway station shortly after landing on the beach and sent to a POW camp. It is believed there were other more successful landings of spies along the St. Lawrence coast.

The worst loss of life occurred on the night of November 24, when the corvette HMCS Shawinigan was sunk a few miles off Port aux Basque. Ninety-one crew members died that night including former Toronto Maple leaf hockey player Dudley "Red" Garrett.

It finally ended in May of 1945 when two German submarines surrendered to the RCN at Bay Bulls, Newfoundland and Sherburne, Nova Scotia and the war was over.

Today, a monument bearing the names of all the seamen who lost their lives in the Battle of the St. Lawrence has a place of prominence on the Halifax Harbour Boardwalk.

OF GRIZZLY BEARS AND POWS

Most of the some 35,000 German prisoners who sat out part of WWII in Canadian POW camps thought they had it pretty good. So good that many Canadians in nearby towns claimed the inmates were eating better than they were. So good that when the War ended, officers had to check under beds and in closets for prisoners who didn't want to be shipped back to Germany. So good that many of the prisoners later returned to Canada to live.

But there are always those for whom good is never quite good enough. During the four years or so that enemy combatants were guests in our Country two escapes were successful out of 600 attempts.

Sometimes the escapees were caught by guards or police. In one notorious case, all it took was a grizzly bear to send a pack of escapees scuttling back to the safety of barbed wire and armed guards. It's a hilarious story really!

To be honest, life at Camp Ozada isn't all that great so it's hard to blame the men for wanting to get out. Built as a temporary camp until the permanent one at Lethbridge is finished, Ozada is nothing but 3,400 tents jammed into a field in the foothills of the Rockies about 80 miles west of Calgary. No fun under canvas in the cold and wet of a Canadian fall and winter.

Since the camp is essentially in the middle of nowhere, security is very lax, so it takes no great effort for a small band of prisoners to cut a hole through the barbed wire one night and head for the hills. The hills in this case, of course, being the Rocky Mountains.

Their research seems a bit foggy here. We don't know how they plan to scale the mountains but the one thing we do know is they haven't planned on the grizzly bear rearing up in front of them. Never having seen anything like an angry giant bear before, the men let out whoops of fear and do a rapid about face!

Word is, the guards welcome the badly shaken group back into Ozada the next morning with more than a few chuckles and when the "bear scare" stories make the rounds, there are no more escape attempts anywhere near the Rockies!

OPERATION KIEBITZ

It's the fall of 1943, things are not going well for the mighty German war machine. The invasion of Russia is turning into a disaster, they've lost North Africa, the Allies are on the march in Sicily and Italy, the once fearsome U-boats are taking heavy losses in the Atlantic, German cities are being blow apart by Allied bombing. One of the things desperately needed is some good news, some hope, a morale booster.

The Kruegsmarine (German Navy) decides to launch a bold plan to rescue four war heroes from the Prisoner of War Camp near Bowmanville, Ontario. A plan they call "Operation Kiebitz". The four, Horst Elfe, Captain of the U-boat U-93, Hans Ey, captain of U-433, Otto Kretschmer, captain of U-99 and Hans Joachim Knebel-Doberitz, Executive Officer of U-99 are top U-boat "Aces". Knebel-Dobertiz is the former adjutant of Admiral Karl Donitz. Their rescue would provide sensational propaganda.

The plan is for the four to tunnel their way out of Camp 30 near Bowmanville, make their way to rendezvous with a U-boat at Pointe de Maisonnette on Chaleur Bay in the St. Lawrence in late September of 1943.

All instructions are sent by coded messages through the International Red Cross. What they don't know is that Canadian authorities are fully aware of the plans and instead of putting a stop to it they implement an audacious "sting" operation.

The prisoners at Camp 30 dig several tunnels, one of which collapses and the four "aces" have to be caught or the enemy will be tipped off that their coded messages are being understood by Canadian authorities.

But another U-boat officer, Wolfgang Heyda is allowed to escape and make his way to the rendezvous spot at Pointe de Maisonette. To make sure the Germans don't suspect anything, police make a great show of trying to catch Heyda while always knowing exactly where he is.

The idea is, of course, to lure the rescue U-boat to the pick-up point then move in and make a spectacular capture.

To make sure they get their boat, the Royal Canadian Navy and the Canadian Army establish a portable surface radar unit on shore at the Pointe de Maisonnette lighthouse.

Hidden in a nearby cove are HMCS Rimouski and several other warships ready to pounce.

Heyda is arrested at the site. A signal light flashes the correct code (thanks to those deciphered codes) and they wait breathlessly for the submarine to surface and pull into shore.

Very clearly they are not breathless enough. The U-536 arrives at the pick-up point as scheduled on the night of September 26, 1943 but the captain is suspicious. His hydrophones pick up some strange noises from the Canadian task force nearby. He remains submerged and manages to evade the war ships and their depth charges.

The four U-boat "aces" finish the war at Bowmanville's camp 30, but U-536 is sunk the following month near the Azores by one British and two Canadian warships. All 38 aboard die.

THE AVRO ARROW MYSTERY

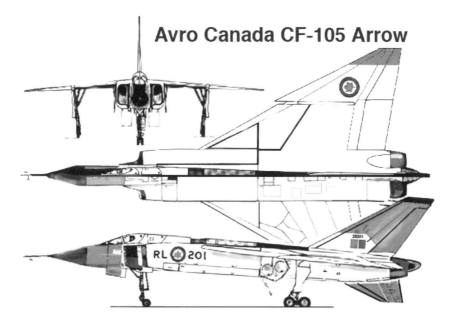

Avro Canada CF-105 Arrow

Did one Avro Arrow survive Black Friday? Did they really totally wipe the best aircraft Canada ever built from the face of the earth? Is there still one out their hiding in someone's barn? The rumours certainly persist!

A few years ago a man claiming to have been an engineer who worked for Avro Canada called my show on CFRB in Toronto. "I know for a fact," he claimed, "that not all of the CF-105 Arrows were destroyed on Black Friday when Diefenbaker scrapped the program." I pressed him further. "Yes," he said, "when the order came down to destroy all of the planes, the five that had been test flying were cut up and the parts sold for scrap. But there was a 6th that was about 95 per cent finished construction. I can tell you, that plane was not cut up, it just very mysteriously disappeared overnight, not an easy task but I swear this is true!"

I couldn't get any more information from him but he certainly sounded legitimate.

And that's not the only clue that one of these supersonic marvels may have survived.

One of the claims made by several of those involved was that Air Marshall W.A. Curtiss a World War I "ace" who headed Avro, ignored Diefenbaker's orders and spirited one of the Arrows away to be saved for posterity.

In 1968, long after Black Friday when Curtiss was asked point blank if he had saved one of the craft he responded: "I don't want to answer that." Then he proceeded to question whether it would be safe to reveal the existence of such a plane. "If it is in existence it may have to wait another ten years. Politically it may cause a lot of problems," are his exact words!

This we do know for sure. The nosecone of Avro Arrow RL-206 was smuggled out of the Avro Aircraft Plant in Malton by members of the RCAF Flying Personnel Medical Establishment. We know it exits because there it is on display today at the Canada Aviation and Space Museum in Ottawa!

The commanding officer of the Medical Establishment Wing Commander Ray Stubbbs explains:

"One day, after a change of government, the new RCAF Chief of Air Staff came to inspect our facilities and programs and after lunch, I asked if he would like to see something special. I showed him a piece of the Arrow cockpit section and engine nacelles and a few other bits. I asked him what we should do with it and he said keep it hidden until the climate in Ottawa was right and then he would arrange to have it placed in the National Aeronautical Museum in Ottawa. Eventually this was done and at least a little bit of history was saved".

Whether a complete or nearly complete Arrow survived Black Friday or not, there is no question it was a marvel of engineering. Not only the best aircraft ever built in Canada, with a top speed almost double that of sound, but at the time of its construction it was the most advanced interceptor aircraft in the world.

It was designed during the Cold War to intercept and shoot down long range bombers which in 1953 were the main form of anticipated nuclear attack. But by the time the Arrow came off the assembly lines in 1958, the main danger was not from bombers, but intercontinental nuclear tipped missiles.

The Diefenbaker Government decided to scrap the Arrow project and instead allow the Americans to install "Bomarc" missiles in the Canadian north. When Diefenbaker refused to allow the Bomarcs to be equipped with nuclear weapons it created a great uproar both in Canada and the United States.

The Conservatives lost the 1963 election and the incoming Liberals immediately armed the Bomarcs with nuclear warheads, but that's another story.

Black Friday, the day Diefenbaker ordered the destruction of all Arrows, was February 20, 1958. More than 24,000 workers lost their jobs; many of the Arrow engineers fled south and began working for the NASA space program.

If you have any information concerning the possible existence of an Avro Arrow, or part of one, please let me know. I don't think the chapter has been completely closed yet!

SAVING BABIES

We can thank the famous Canadarm for helping to save the lives of tiny babies. More than that, we can thank the Canadarm for the development of technology that is revolutionizing medical practice in many different theatres.

It all began back in 1975 when the Canadian National Research Council and NASA signed an agreement that Canada would take part in the Space Shuttle program by developing and constructing a shuttle remote-controlled "manipulator" system.

What resulted was a marvel of engineering—a remote-controlled mechanical arm, not unlike a human arm with wrist, elbow and shoulder. Each of the three joints allowed what we called the Canadarm, to bend and turn with even more flexibility than a human arm. What isn't generally known is that five Canadarms were built.

The very first flight was with the space shuttle Columbia on November 13, 1981. The Canadarm performed beautifully, exceeding all design goals.

Between 1981 and 2011, when the Space Shuttle Program ended, the Canadarm flew on 91 different missions. Sadly one of those missions was the ill-fated Challenger which exploded shortly after takeoff.

The remaining four flew 90 highly successful missions, among other things repairing satellites, positioning astronauts and maintaining equipment. Some of their more famous accomplishments were helping to repair the Hubble Space Telescope, docking the Internal Space Station to the Russian Mir

Space Station, knocking off ice that was blocking a waste exit on the shuttle and best known of all, helping to construct the International Space Station.

But the Canadarm technology didn't die in 2011 when the shuttles were retired.

The next generation of the Canadarm is Canadarm 2, the Space Station "manipulator" system, a bigger smarter version of the original. It played a major part in the construction of the Space Station and is still up there conducting maintenance, supporting astronauts working in space and handling payloads.

As the robotic technology improved, a new even more sophisticated piece of equipment was added to the Space Station. It's called a "Special Purpose Dexterous Manipulator" (Dextre). It uses the same technology as the Canadarm and is essentially a robot handyman used for a wide range of tasks. Each gripper on "Dextre" has sensors that give it a human-like sense of touch as well as retractable tools, a camera, lights and a retractable umbilical connector to provide power and data connections when the robot manipulates electronic equipment and conducts experiments.

It is this "Dextre" technology that is now being developed at Toronto's SickKids Hospital to build a new robot capable of performing delicate procedures on little patients more accurately and faster than a surgeon's hands. This new application of Canadian space technology promises to pave the way for new pediatric surgical tools that will make procedures safer and less invasive.

The third version of the robot is now being tested and shows promising applications for fetal, neurological, cardiac, and urological surgeries.

There is even later news concerning Canadarm technology. The Centre for Surgical Innovation and Invention is now using Canadarm technology to develop an image-guided autonomous robot which they believe may improve our ability to diagnose and treat patients with a high risk of breast cancer.

THE LAST GOOD YEAR

When the ebullient little Mayor of Montreal, Jean Drapeau, tries to promote Expo 67, in the fall of 1966, my radio listeners tear him to shreds. Or would have had he been a lesser man!

"You're a damn fool! You'll bankrupt the Country! That crazy World's Fair you're talking about will embarrass us all. The islands you're building will sink!" All typical of the comments that pour into my show on CFRA, Ottawa.

None of it seems to phase Drapeau. "I've heard it all before many times," he says and keeps smiling.

Before he leaves the studio he hands me a special invitation to attend the opening ceremonies for Expo 67, April 27, 1967. "That's six months from now," he says with a vigorous hand shake. "We will amaze the world!"

It's about a year later when he bounces into my studio, sits down in front of a microphone and clamps on the earphones.

What a difference a year makes! The praise, the joy, the pride that floods into those earphones has him up out of his chair, literally dancing on more than one occasion.

Some callers are so ecstatic they are almost crying. "I've never been so proud to be Canadian! Uplifting! Spirit lifting! A great achievement! Thank you so much Mr. Drapeau! One of the happiest times our family has ever experienced! God bless you Mayor Drapeau, please run for Prime Minister!" All typical reactions from a very grateful and proud City.

And not just Ottawa. Praise pours in from around the world. It is undoubtedly the greatest World's Fair in history. Its success will never be repeated.

Pierre Berton in his book, "The Last Good Year", calls the Fair "a miracle, one of the shining moments in this nation's history!"

Peter C. Newman writes: "It's the greatest thing we ever did as a nation. It's the sun, the moon and the stars!"

The New York Times is highly laudatory as is much of the world's press. The Times Architecture critic, Ada Louise Huxtable, has special praise for the Quebec pavilion saying: "The Quebec pavilion combines an exceptionally refined work of contemporary architecture with an exhibition design that is a three-dimensional sensory abstraction of sight and electronic sound that says, quite suddenly and stunningly what a 1967 exhibit should be!"

Expo 67—Man and His World--is there anyone who attended who does not recall the pride, the joy, the downright amazement that this country, Canada, could do something this fantastic?

Sixty-two nations, 90 pavilions, some of which are awe-inspiring, four of which are still in use. (La Ronde, Quebec's largest amusement park, the Geodesic Dome U.S. Pavilion now dedicated to the environment, the French and Quebec Pavilions now transformed into Casino de Montreal and of course the famous Habitat 67, 354 identical cubes artfully stacked to make 148 apartments).

The most optimistic projection was for a total attendance of 30 million. In fact when Man and his World closes on October 29, total attendance is 50,306,648! That doesn't include the staff or special permits.

More than 200,000 attend the first day. More than 569,000 pour through the gates the third day, an all-time one day attendance record at a world's fair.

Total cost to three levels of government, Montreal, Quebec and Federal--$283 million.

Total revenue, including tourism, attributed to the Fair—$480 million.

The joy and pride it gives the nation—priceless!

SUMMING UP

I don't recall the date. Sometime in the mid to late 80's I'm playing golf with Al Saikali, owner of Ottawa's best steak house, Billy Joe, owner of several restaurants and other businesses in the Capital and Lorry Greenberg, former Mayor of Ottawa.

We're having a great time. I do remember it was a beautiful day, early fall and the Hunt Club fairways are in far better shape than my game. I'm especially getting a kick out of the bets being tossed about by Al and Billy. They're playing a game called bingo, bango, bongo. Ten bucks for the longest drive, another tenner for first on the green, and yet another ten for first down the hole.

It's far too rich for me and Lorry pleads a bad back.

The two combatants are hard at it. Dropping a club just as his opponent draws back his driver, a coughing fit as a putt is being lined up, loud claims the other guy moved his ball out of a divot. If you've ever played with guys like this you get the drift. Lots of laughs, boasts and some pretty awful golf.

As we approach the 18th it begins to dawn on me!

Here I am, out here on the prestigious Hunt Club golf course with a guy who arrived as a young man from Lebanon, holes in his shoes, can't speak English or French, starts out washing dishes in a bowling alley and now owns a very successful restaurant and goodness knows what else.

Playing him for as much as $30 a hole is a guy from very humble beginnings who has overcome heaven only knows what discrimination to become a leading member of Ottawa's Chinese Community and a very successful businessman.

And riding in my cart, the man who became Ottawa's first Jewish mayor.

And me, a guy raised on a hardscrabble Ontario farm with pump-your-own water, coal oil lamps and an outdoor privy.

So I'm thinking to myself.

IS THIS A GREAT COUNTRY OR WHAT!?

CANADA 150